Immediate RELEASE

Escaping the Allure of the Game

MR. B

Book Cover Design: Prize Publishing House

Printed by: Prize Publishing House, LLC in the United States of America.

First printing edition 2023.

Prize Publishing House
P.O. Box 9856, Chesapeake, VA 23321
www.PrizePublishingHouse.com

Library of Congress Control Number: 2023916543

ISBN (Paperback): 979-8-9884324-6-3
ISBN (E-Book): 979-8-9884324-7-0`

CONTENTS

FOREWORD

Brandon's story is real, gritty, and raw. It is a story of a kid from a single-parent home who was influenced by his surroundings. It is a tale of a bigger plan and finding out that you concealed greatness. Brandon never stopped fighting and planning in the fight of his trials and tribulations. If I had to describe the phrase "Never let the torch go out," it would reference Brandon Harrington.

I roamed the same danger zones and flocked the same drug-spirited locations as Brandon, so change and a lender would be an understatement. Brandon's character, only a few, can tell a story of corruption, power, and greed, and it's really a true story experienced by a young man, 21 years old, from a small country town.

— **Tony Horne- Former NFL Player and XXXIV Super Bowl Champ**

1

PASSION TO WIN

I was told that I was a miracle child because my mom conceived me while her tubes were tied. I never knew what that meant as a child, but over the years, I realized that I was destined to be here. I was the youngest of three kids. During the early stages of my parent's marriage, they didn't think they could have kids, so they adopted my older cousin and raised him as their own. About five years later, my mom became pregnant with my older brother Brian, and then four years later, Brandon, the miracle baby, was born. My mom would later tell me that, at the age of one, she put a basketball in my hand. As far back as I can remember, I kept that basketball in my hand throughout my adolescence. I fell in love with the game of basketball. I can honestly say basketball was my first true love, or at least I thought it was. Basketball was the first game I learned, but the competitiveness I was born with made me work hard to perfect the craft. As far back as I can remember, I hated to lose in anything I did. I will never forget sitting down with my aunt Joanne, my mom's older sister. When I was around five, she asked me what I wanted to be when I grew up. Of course, I told her I wanted to go to the NBA. It was her response that would stick with me for the rest of my days, though. She told me, "Brandon, whatever you decide to be, you make sure that you are the best at it. And always be a leader and never be a follower." For whatever reason, as a five-year-old child, that conversation with my aunt stuck with me. I started to really study the game of basketball. I would watch the film of the great players like Larry Bird, Michael Jordan, and Isaiah Thomas. I really watched the smaller guys in the league, like Spud Webb and Mugsy Bogues, because I was short like them, and I knew I had to be tough like them if I wanted to make it in basketball, being that I was so short. My aunt's statement about being a leader and never a follower would be a nugget that I always carried with me and would be why I wanted to be the one who stood out when I walked into a room. Not vocally but just my presence alone.

Being a leader stuck with me from a child. I never just took things off face value. You couldn't just tell me things without me asking questions like why and what for before I did it. I got a lot of whoopings for talking back, which is what the older folks called it back then, but it had to make sense to me before I did it. All through school, that passion for winning, being the best at what I'm doing, and that nugget from my aunt to be a leader and not a follower was what I lived life by. I kept good grades throughout school because I was determined to be my best at whatever I did, including school.

As a kid, I spent a lot of time with my mom's brother

Coy. It would be my Uncle Coy who would introduce me to my first hustle. A legitimate hustle, that is. My uncle lived about an hour west of us in nearby Charlotte, N.C., but he would come home every weekend to sell merchandise at the local flea market every Saturday, and I would go with him as his little helper, and he would pay me twenty dollars for helping him. Mind you, I was always asking questions. It was just something I always did. So when this became a regular thing, I started to ask my uncle where he got all this merchandise from. He would literally have everything from men's and women's clothes to house appliances and shoes. You name it, and he damn near had it in that van. It would be then when my uncle started giving me the game on how to flip the money that I was making with him. He told me to save the money he was paying me, and when the summer came, I could stay with him, and he would show me how to make money.

So I saved my little money up, and when the summer came, sure enough, he took me to Charlotte with him and introduced me to his hustle. He showed how he went to different thrift stores in the city where the rich folks would donate brand-new merchandise, and he would buy it for cheap and come back down to the country and sell it with a markup. For example, he would get a Tommy Hilfiger jacket for ten dollars from the thrift stores and turn around and sell it for forty dollars. During this summer is when he showed me how to really hustle. It was crazy because I was only around eight, but learning this intrigued me. That summer, I went to Charlotte with like a hundred dollars, and I invested it all.

So when we went back to the flea market, and I sold all of my merchandise, I was sold on the hustle. That passion to win was again tickled. I would hustle with my uncle like this off and on until I became a teenager.

Coming up as a kid, I was really the leader out of my friends, even though I was the younger one. My house was the hang-out for us because, coming up, my parents spoiled my brothers and me with everything we wanted. I was blessed to have a black top right in my backyard. All the kids in my hood and the hood a block over called Chapel Town came to my house to play basketball. Chapel Town, which is called Chap for short, was the hood for real. There were several juke joints on every corner back then, and drugs were being sold on every corner along with prostitutes. Somebody was always being beaten, shot, stabbed, or killed back then, so my dad didn't allow us to hang out with any of our friends over there. Being that I wasn't allowed to hang out in Chap, all my friends that lived there would walk to my house, where we would play basketball all day and night when there wasn't school the next day. There were always some three-on-three or four-on-four basketball games going on at my house. Mind you, I was four years younger than my brother Brian and almost ten years younger than my adopted brother. At the age of seven or eight, I was getting picked up to play three-on-three with my older brother and his friends.

I was never one to let size or age intimidate me in anything since I could remember because in everything that I did, I made sure I was my best at it, and I worked hard to make sure my game spoke for me so I didn't have to. I played little league basketball at the local parks and rec, and I was something to be reckoned with. I can honestly say that no one my age could stand in front of my game. The gym would be packed on the nights I played because everyone wanted to see the show that I put on. But to me, I was just trying to win. And winning is what I did and became accustomed to ever since I could remember.

Fast forward to the early '90s. This would be the era when crack cocaine was tearing up Black families in the urban community. Around this time would be when my mom caught my dad cheating with a close friend of hers. This would be the beginning of a traumatic change in my life. This was when the allure of the game began. I had never seen my mom and dad argue at all, but after my mom caught my dad with her friend, I began to see them argue and fight. For the next few months, I would witness a lot of fighting. I remember one day, my mom took me and my brother to ride with her somewhere; we didn't know where we were going, but when we got to the destination, it was a hotel. The hotel was where the lady worked that my mom had caught with my dad. So when we got there, my mom told us to sit in the car while she confronted this lady about sleeping with her husband. I vividly remember my mom walking up the steps to the second floor of this hotel. When she got to the room where she had spotted the lady she was looking for cleaning, she approached her, and I could see them exchanging words. Before you knew it, my mom had this lady by her neck and was about to throw her over the balcony of this hotel. My brother instantly jumped out of the car and ran upstairs full speed to pull my mom off the lady. Had it not been for my brother, my mom probably would have caught a murder charge that day. This was all new to me; I just couldn't wrap my mind around what was taking place, but I knew things were about to be different.

By the time I was ten, my parents had gotten a divorce. My mom never had to take care of the household bills while she and my dad were together, so her being the head of the household now would be new for us and her as well. Being without my dad, my mom had to learn how to hold the house down on her own, which put a lot of stress on her; my brother and I could tell. After my parents split, my mom wasn't the same. I could see the hurt and embarrassment on my mom's face, but she was determined not to fail us. I always was ahead of my time, but with what my mom was facing, my brother and I felt we had to step up and help her. Looking back at it today, I realize that the passion for winning came from my mom because I saw her pull it together fast and make a way for my brother and me.

At ten years old, I started learning about finances. I learned how to help her manage the money and pay bills. I learned about checking and savings accounts. I learned how to balance a checkbook, what credit cards were, and how they worked. Things did get rough for us for a little while. However, my mom came from a tight-knit family, and her siblings were there to help. We were used to having everything that we wanted. My dad still came around and made sure he paid my mom child support, but he was busy trying to rebuild his new life just like my mom, so he didn't have much extra time to give, just like my mom.

My mom had started working the third shift, and around this time, my cousin Caleb moved in with us to be our babysitter during the night. Caleb was about twelve years older than me and like eight years older than my brother. He was the son of my mom's sister and had just come back from college with his eyes set on the drug game. Caleb took over fairly quickly because before you knew it, I would be watching Caleb, my mom, and our uncle count trash bags of money sitting at my mom's kitchen table. I started to look up to Caleb because I appreciated how he helped my mom out. By this time, my brother Brian had already begun to hang in the streets and try his hand in the drug game with his best friend, Blaze. They were barely going to school and catching cases for breaking and entering, so Caleb decided to let them make some money with him. I was still going to school and getting good grades. I wasn't thinking about selling drugs. However, I did have a hustle going on. I would convince my homeboy Ant to get his cousin to take us to school every morning. I would have him take us by the store every morning to steal all the best packs of gum and candies, and we would take them to school to sell. We sold so much of it until word got back to the principal that kids weren't eating at the middle school because they were spending all their lunch money with me and my boy Ant. So he stopped us coming in one morning and popped us with our book bags filled with candy and gum one morning. He took all our candy that day and banned us from selling candy at school. I couldn't stand the fact that I had gotten popped. And that passion to win just wouldn't let me allow that principal to stop my hustle.

Through middle school, I continued to play basketball and get good grades. My parents didn't seem to support me much anymore because they were busy trying to rebuild their lives without each other. Financially, my dad still supported us, but because of work and living in another state over in South Carolina, he wasn't present much anymore. My mom was always tired and sleeping due to her third shift job, so she didn't want to be bothered much when she was home.

Mom never got over the hurt from catching my dad with her friend. I don't know if it was the hurt from the betrayal from her friend or my dad, but I do know that it scared her, and because of it, she didn't want my brother and me to have friends. We could go with family anytime, but friends were another thing. She had reached the point that I couldn't have friends over to play basketball anymore. I think that's when I started losing my passion for my first love, basketball, and started admiring the drug game. At this point, I started to hang with my older cousin Ron. Our mothers were first cousins, and he wasn't but about six years older than me. He was now out on his own and head first in the dope game, but my mom would let me go with him whenever I wanted. My cousin Ron is where I got my toughness from. Before I started hanging out with him, he would always come by my mom's house to see us and always challenged me to a game of one-on-one basketball. He would make large bets to me, like one hundred dollars to my nothing if I could beat him. Man, my cousin would literally be hitting me with real elbows, pushing me down and all, and I couldn't call foul. Man, it would be tough playing him, but I would win some of those bets, quite a few, I may add because I was born with that passion to win. No matter how much he would try and beat me up to discourage me not to win, it didn't stop me from making the proper adjustments to put me in a position to win, even though I was taking an ass whooping doing it.

After the split between my parents, it seemed like I went from watching sports with my dad to watching gangster movies with my big brothers and cousins. When I started watching them, I was intrigued by the power that everyone gained when they became rich. That was what I saw that they all had in common, from the mobsters like John Gotti, Bumpy Johnson, Scarface, King of New York, and Nino Brown. Another thing they all had in common was they all were leaders! Outside of school, I rarely hung out with any of my friends because now I was hanging out with the older guys in the neighborhood that were getting money. I wasn't hustling, but I was learning. I was watching and observing. Taking it all in, even their mistakes. I did have one friend that I hung with that was my age at the time. That friend was Spence. He wasn't from South Park, the neighborhood I grew up in. His family moved there when I was around nine, and we became tight. He was the youngest of three kids and rebellious. His parents were still together, but he was just a troublemaker. I used to try and talk him out of a lot of the things he was doing, but it rarely worked. Nobody really liked him in the hood because it was always a fight when he was around. I was the only one that could kinda control him. I did have two more friends that I knew before Spence, who I was real tight with,

Ant and Jr. They were my aces, but we rarely got to hang out because they had no freedom to roam like I did.

Ant and I only hung out when he came to spend the weekend with his grandma in South Park. His mom was like my mom, a single parent, but she didn't let Ant do shit when we were coming up. Jr stayed with his grandparents. They were older and set in their ways. They didn't let Jr go anywhere, either. Jr and I had a strange relationship because his mom was the friend that got caught with my dad. My mom didn't want us being friends at all. In the beginning of all the mess with our parents, it affected our relationship. We even fought at some point about it, but it never came between our friendship. My everyday friend back then was Spence, and he introduced me to his friend he knew before he moved to South Park named Tom, but everybody called him Thug Life. Thug Life was a live wire. We were always getting into something. Neither of us was into selling drugs yet, but they would like to steal cars, motorcycles, and shit. I wasn't into that stealing shit. I was a hustler. I was into turning one to two and three to six, all by using my mind. That stealing shit was something different, and it wasn't me.

2

LOVE OF THE GAME

At the age of 13 is when I really started sneaking hustling crack. I wasn't in the streets with it, but I would steal it from my brother and sell it all to my next-door neighbor, Dodirty. Dodirty was the handyman of my neighborhood that lived next door with his mother. Dodirty was one of those guys that was a real player back in his day and had some things going on. He was a mechanic by trade and once had his own shop, a nice house, and a beautiful family, but he played around with the rock and lost it all. He had a damn good soul and was like family to me because he had known me since I was a baby. When I started sneaking selling dope, it was Dodirty that I would give it to, and he would pay me when he got paid on Friday. It would be on these Fridays when he got paid that I would hang out with him in the storage building on the back of his mom's house, where he hung out and listened to R&B and soul music while he got high, drunk forties, and worked on cars as a side hustle.

Dodirty would tell me a bunch of stories from back in the 70s when cocaine became the thing to do in the urban community. He would tell me all about his ups and downs. It would be on one of those Fridays when he would tell me, "The most dangerous thing in this world is them four letters!" I looked at him and said, "What four letters?" while thinking in my head that Dodirty was high as hell. He would tell me the four letters he is talking about is "LOVE." He would say, "A man will kill you over LOVE." He then said, "See, you can take a man's money, but if that man is not in love with money, then it really will not be a thing. But if that man loves that money, then he will kill you for it and vice versa." He would say, "It's the same way about a man and his woman. If he's deeply in love with that woman, then he will kill you over that woman or for her." See, it all made sense. It's the love of the things that come from the game that gets you killed. If not physically, it will mentally.

By the time I was 14, I had fallen in love with the game for real. The drug game, that is. I had sat around and taken notes for the past four years. The same way I had sat around and watched my favorite NBA player play when I was in love with the game of basketball. Now, I had studied all the drug dealers and watched how they had made their mistakes, so I knew what not to do and what to do. I had been stealing crack and money from my older brother for the past few years without him knowing. He had heard it in the streets and approached me a few times about it. One time, in particular, was in this hood that I had started hustling in when I was in my ninth grade. The name of the hood was Long Drive. By the time I started my tenth-grade year, I had become tight as hell with one of my brother's homeboys named Black. He was the youngest out of my brother's crew, so quite naturally, he and I were tight because we were closer in age. The summer before my tenth-grade year, we really got to hang tight, making moves together. Hell, we even hit my brother's stash together and took like five pounds of weed the summer before my tenth-grade year. So that whole tenth-grade year, I rode to school with Black, and after school, I would have him drop me off on Long Drive, called The Drive for short. I would post up with a few of the guys on The Drive that I was cool with and hustle weed.

This day when I was out there, I was with my man Flint posted in front of the apartment, chilling, waiting for sales to pull up. Flint was my nigga. Flint was originally from New Jersey and had moved down south to live with his grandmother. I don't know how we became so tight, but we did, and we became students of the game together. My brother rolled down on us this particular day. He pulled up and got out and pulled me to the side, and said, "What you doing over here, Brandon?" I'm like, "Man, I'm over here with my man Flint about to shoot some dice." He then said, "I hear you out here running to cars selling weed and shit." I say to him, "Man, go ahead; you are tripping." He then starts to pat my pockets and shaking me down, asking me where the weed is. "You better not be out here bullshitting!" His search came up empty, so he hopped back into his truck and pulled off. Little did he know I had learned from his mistakes not to have shit on me for the police or the stick-up kids to get it off me. I had my sack of dime bags stuffed in the bush in an empty potato chip bag. That's why when he emptied my pockets, he only saw that I had like two hundred dollars in my pockets, which was normal for me to have on me at that age. The thing was, I studied him and all my older cousins that were in the game years before me. I listened to the stories hanging around the older folks like my mom and uncles and listened to stories about this dope dealer and that dope dealer getting busted and how or how this dope dealer got robbed. So I soaked that all in because I had found love for the drug game.

I had been a hustler since a child, hustling at the flea market selling merchandise. But now I had become infatuated with hustling drugs and the thrill to outdo the ones before me and to become the best at it. Hustling had become a passion, so much so to the point that I would leave school every day at lunch and go hit the block. And on the days I did that, I wouldn't go back to school, and my grades had begun to reflect that too. Which was odd to my mom because even though I was in the streets doing shit, I always kept good grades. The only days I stayed the whole day in school was when I knew I could get my sacks off at school, which was mostly after school. So if I had enough sales lined up after school, I would just stay and get scraps off the students who wanted weed. I had gotten a name for myself for selling weed in school so much until one day, I had driven my mom's car to school, and it just so happened I was in ISS this day. So I parked the car and, like always, had my sack of dime bags in an empty potato chip bag. So when I got out of the car, I made sure no one was watching, and like always, I dropped the potato chip bag on the ground and then kicked the bag under the car parked next to where I parked. Once I did that, I walked to the ISS classroom. Not even an hour later, the school police and principal walked into the ISS classroom and randomly searched everyone. In my mind, I knew this wasn't just a random search of the classroom. I had never heard of them doing this before. However, I was the last student they took out of the classroom to search. So when they brought me outside, they did a pat search on my person, which came up empty, and then the principal and the school officer looked at me and said, "Brandon, where is the marijuana?" I looked at them and said, "What are you guys talking about? I don't have any weed!" So, at this point, they had already had this bust planned. Little did I know they knew I had driven that day, so at this point, they walked me back to the parking lot where I had parked, and they had the K9 dog from the sheriff's department there when I got to the parking lot. They put the dog all in my mom's car but came up empty. The whole time I was talking shit, telling them someone had given them some false information. At the end of this clown show, they told me they would be watching me. But they did make me get someone else to drive my mom's car from school because my young ass didn't have any license. I'm just glad they didn't call my mom because, hell, she didn't even know I had her car. Looking back now, it was the thrill of the chase that my young mind liked as well. Outsmarting the opposition had become a thrill, as well as making the money.

It didn't take long before my mom saw that I was heading down the same road as my older brother and cousins. My grades started to reflect that I wasn't going to school. So my mom decided to send me to stay with my dad in Chesterfield, S.C. However, by now, I was in love with the game. I was sick that I had to go and stay with my dad and leave my friends behind, but most of all, I hated that the move would put brakes to my hustle. I also didn't want to leave my then-girlfriend named Jada. In the days leading up to my leaving to go stay with my dad, I went by to see my big cousin Ron to let him know my mom was making me move down south with my dad. After talking with Ron, I didn't feel so bad. The biggest thing about me moving with my dad was not being able to hustle, but during that conversation with my cousin, he told me, "Lil cuz, it's money everywhere, and we can beat all prices down in South Carolina. You are a born hustler, so you can get money anywhere you go."

When I left my cousin that day, I was ready to embark on South Carolina. The day came real quick for me to move. So when my dad came, I wanted to make one stop before we left, and that was to Jada's house to see her before I left. Even though where I was moving to was only 45 minutes away, it felt like I was going across the country and I would never see her again. So my dad dropped me off for a few hours to spend with her before we made our way to South Carolina. Once there, I settled into my room, looked around, and instantly got sick. My dad stayed off in the country for real. Houses were miles apart from each other in the middle of nowhere, it seemed. The next day my dad took me to enroll in school at Cheraw High. This high school was extremely small compared to the high school back home. I was a little nervous because I didn't know anyone. The next day, I started school. When I walked in, the first person I saw was one of my homeboys from back home. His name was BG. BG was from Chap. His dad had a little league football team in the hood that we all played on in elementary. They had moved away during elementary school back in the day, but I didn't know they had moved here to Cheraw. BG was in the twelfth grade, and I was just in the tenth, but he quickly put me in the loop of who was who at the school. He would be the one that would introduce me to BDot, who would become my partner in crime during my time staying in S.C and thereafter.

BDot was a year older than me. He already had his license and a car. BDot and I became extremely close. We both loved to chase behind the girls. That was something that we both had in common. BDot wasn't into the hustling, but he knew all the fellas at the school that were, and he was cool with them. So, naturally, I became cool with them as well. Once I became cool with them, I started asking what they were paying for their weed. When I found out the prices they were paying, I was baffled because they were paying twice what I could get the weed for. Once I found that out, I knew I was about to put my foot down in this town.

The arrangement between my parents was to stay with my dad and go to school with him, and I come to stay with my mom on the weekends. However, once I moved in with my dad, my mom decided to move in with my uncle and rent her house out so that she could get ahead. She felt that it was the best move being that she was staying alone after I moved with my dad. My uncle lived next door to my cousin Ron's mom, so when I would come home on the weekends, I spent most of that time with my cousin Ron. It was crazy because the way that I hung up under my cousin Ron is the way that my brother hung up under Ron's older brother, Dave. It would be Ron that I started getting my weed from to supply the guys down south. We came up with an operation where he gave me the keys to his stash house so whenever I needed to re-up, all I had to do was have my man BDot bring me to his house, and even if he wasn't home, I could get what I needed and leave the money there for him to get. The operation was sweet, and I instantly started making moves down south. The first fella I began to do business with down south on the hustling tip was Slim. Slim was a year older than me, but Bro was getting bread, and eventually, through him, I would meet other guys that were getting money like him who wanted to do business with me. He started off buying half pounds from me every week. I would get the whole pound for $600 and sell him half for the same $600, leaving me a free half of a pound that I would then bust in half and front out to my man Jay and CDog, who would move that for me every week. It seemed like every week my guys started to sell more and more. Before I knew it, I was selling five to ten pounds a week in the tenth grade. The more I sold, the less my profit was because the more they bought, the more I would drop the price. It wasn't about the profit margin with me. It was more about consistency. It was cool if I made only two hundred dollars off each pound as long as I sold five or ten pounds that week.

As I started to get money down south, I also started to have more females on my line, which brought about a lot of hate from the guys in this little town. The hate got so real that I had to tell my cousin Ron. When I told Ron about the hate I was getting from these guys, he gave me two pistols to take down south with me. One was a 22 mini revolver I could carry everywhere in my shoes, and the other was a 38 special snub nose. He made it clear not to play with anyone who tried to harm me, and I wasn't about to let anybody do any harm to me. BDot was with all the bullshit I was on, but he just didn't know anything about hustling. True indeed, he was soaking it all up from me, but he wasn't ready to hustle, and I didn't try to force him into it. He was good if I was good. It didn't take long before I started to get into trouble with the law down south. The first charge I caught was for shooting into an occupied dwelling. A lot of the guys down south were really hating on me and the guys that I was running with because we were getting money and had all the girls. This guy who I caught my first case for trying to kill was one. He was in his feelings about a female. This particular day me, BDot, and CDog decided to ride through the projects called ACL in which this fella lived. As we were cruising through, he flagged BDot down, so he stopped. CDog was in the front, and I was in the back with both my guns. When BDot stopped, this fella asked him what we were doing riding through his hood. BDot replied, "Trying to fuck something." So the fella took it upon himself to try and swing on my man BDot, and as soon as he did it, I hung out of the back window and started shooting at him with both of my guns. I don't know how I missed him, but at the end of the day, I was glad. He did rat me out, and I caught my first case down south behind it.

After that incident, it seemed like things just kept happening. Honestly, it wasn't me looking for trouble; it was more so me not backing down from any or ducking out the way of it. I was always just trying to get myself some money and have fun with the girls at this point in my life. I wasn't really saving any money. After about a year, my dad had had enough and took me back to North Carolina with my mom. I really didn't want to leave because I had really gotten used to South Carolina. I had gotten my license that year, and I was making good money selling the weed without having to actually sell it myself. The thing was that I didn't even recognize how deeply I had fallen in love with the game. It wasn't like the streets had chosen me; I had chosen the streets. I was well taken care of by my parents. While I was hustling right under my dad's nose without him knowing it, he would still keep me with money in my pockets and the freshest gear on my back. He even would make sure my homeboy BDot had money in his pockets. However, my dad would always give me speeches about selling drugs because he knew that my brother and all my cousins were drug dealers, and his intention with these conversations was to try and deter me from the path they had chosen. My dad would always tell me that a man selling drugs is no different from a man using drugs because they both are addicted and in love with the drug.

The thing was that my fifteen-year-old mind couldn't understand what he was saying. It wasn't clear to me at the time that a man selling drugs is just as addicted to the drug as the user. See, the allure of the game had me. My mind had become blurred. I was now committed to traveling down the foggy path of life, thinking it was the easy way out. I had started down a road in life that would take me through so many twists and turns to get to where I wanted to be in life. I had a plan, but the route I had chosen to get there would eventually take me extremely long to find my destination, but at this point, I didn't have a clue as to what I was about to endure to get to where I wanted to be. All I knew was that I wanted to be great. I always remembered what my aunt had told me as a little boy: to be the best at whatever it was I wanted to be in life and always be a leader, meaning always control your own destiny. What I didn't know was that the path I had chosen to take would not allow me to control my own destiny. The game had no rules at all. The things you thought you saw, you really didn't. It was the allure of the game that I didn't understand. The allure of the game is what I had seen when I was sitting back watching, being a student of the ones that had come before me. The allure is what the game looked like from the outside but not the inside. The allure is what made the pretty females want to be on the side of a big-time drug dealer, and once they made it beside him, they would fall in love with the game as well. The game seemed like it had a lot to offer, but in actuality, at the end of the day, it had nothing but heartache and pain to offer. I saw many females lose their life, sanity, and peace by just dating men that were in the game.

The game didn't just hurt the person in it, but it also hurt the people associated with the person in the game. The love of the game becomes a drug in itself. We become accustomed to a lifestyle, and with that lifestyle, there is an image that must be maintained. If not, the game will chew you up and spit you out quickly. Unbeknownst to me, I had embarked on a path that would end one or two ways: death or jail. No matter how much I studied the game and told myself that I was going to be the best at it, by design, the game was created to destroy us, the minority, and, most importantly, the Black community. It was way deeper than my teenage mind could fathom, and at this point, I was in love with the game and determined to make a name for myself as one of the greats. I loved the game, or at least I thought I did.

CHAPTER

3

NEVER SHOW YOUR HAND

Even in a little friendly game of spades, one of the number one rules is that you must not show your hand to your opponents! So, in the drug game, just as in this thing called life, we must learn not to show our hand to our opponents at any time, or it will cause us to lose in some way, form, or fashion. By the time I was 13, I had started sneaking into my brother's room, rambling in his hiding places where I knew he kept his drugs and money. Around this time, my brother would have thousands of dollars stashed away in his vent in his room, coat pockets, shoe boxes, and under his mattress. He would also have Ziploc bags full of crack as well. I never touched the crack for a while because I would just take $500 from his stash of cash at a time. I would take a hundred off every thousand-dollar stack until I got my $500 every week. That $500 a week was enough for me to do as I wanted as a teenager. Because there was so much money there, I did not need to take any of the crack. Why risk it for what the crack would bring back anyway – CASH? So, I just rode that wave for a while. After a while, however, he stopped having money at my mom's house like that, but the drugs would be there.

I remember my first time taking some of the crack. I took exactly 15 rocks which was $300 worth back then. I took them out of the Ziploc bag he had stashed in one of his Avirex jackets in his closet. After I took the rocks, I went and found an old ChapStick tube, cleaned it out, and then put my rocks in it like I had seen my older cousins and brother do in the past. I then got myself together and left the house to walk down the road to my homeboy Broady's house. That was like the hangout for everybody in South Park back then. On my way there, I bumped into my old head cousin, Push, who happened to be a crackhead. I knew he was probably heading to Chap to buy him a rock, so I asked him where he was heading, and like I had thought, he was on his way to the hotspot, which was the biggest dope spot in Chap at the time. After he told me where he was going, I asked him what he was going to get. He replied, "Why? Do you have something?" I told him yea, and he told me to sell him a $20 rock. I reached into my pocket, pulled my ChapStick tube out with the rocks in it, and then dumped all fifteen rocks into my hand as if to let him pick which one he wanted. Push looked down into my hand and then back up at me, and before I knew it, he had knocked all my rocks out of my hand and onto the ground. I looked at him and screamed, "What the fuck are you doing?" And then he looked at me and said, "Rule number one, never show your hand. Let alone your whole hand." He went on to say, "I asked you to buy a $20 rock, and you showed me a handful. Never show nobody nothing more than what their money can buy." He then helped me pick all my rocks up off the ground, gave me his twenty-dollar bill, and told me to give him an extra rock for the game he had just given me. That game, I would remember from the streets to the courtroom and also to the boardroom. From that day forward, I stood on that jewel from my cousin Push. I saw many guys get caught up by showing their hands. Some did long prison sentences, some lost it all, and some lost their lives.

Being that I understood not to show my hand early in the game, it was natural for me to throw curves to keep my hands covered but also peep when a hand is being shown and take full advantage of it. That mentality came from the life that I had chosen. It was a dog-eat-dog world, so you had to be on point for all the trick foolery that came with the game. At the age of 17, I was full-fledged in the streets. What did it was my brother going back to prison. See, my brother knew that I was trying to hustle, but he wasn't having it at all. When he found out he was about to go to prison on his second state prison sentence, he sat me down with his best friend Blaze and told me he was about to do a 36-month bid in a few days. He looked at me and then at Blaze and said, "I know my little brother been trying to hustle, and I don't want to go away and leave my brother with no guidance, and I'm not here to protect him, so I want you to show him the ropes to this life we live. Turn him on to where we get it from and who is who for real. Also, show him where to get it off. But most importantly, don't let nothing happen to my brother, Blaze." They dapped and hugged, and Blaze told him he had me.

As promised, me and Blaze became inseparable. He showed me the ins and outs of the game for real. A lot of people don't know how much I learned from Blaze. See, Blaze was the kind of friend that would give you his last. He was a ride-or-die friend for real. I really learned what loyalty was from Blaze. Blaze was cool with everybody, but if you crossed him in any way, his get back was ten times worse than what you did to him. See, he was with all the shit. He taught me that nothing beats the cross but the double cross, but always be looking for the cross so that you are braced for it and you can almost see it coming. No matter how much Blaze had, he always acted like he had nothing. He never showed his hand. By being a student under Blaze, I watched and observed, and learned a lot. See, after soaking up all the game from Blaze, I then started trying to understand why he wasn't on top. He knew all he needed to know to be next level, but he seemed only to go up just to go down and do it all over again. So, I started looking at what he was doing wrong in the game as well. See, I had the mindset that if I'm going to be out here, I will be the very damn best I can be. I learned from Blaze that it was such a thing as being too loyal to friends when it came to the game. Every time Blaze would come up, he looked out for friends that he couldn't turn to for help when he was down. He also loved to party. He never missed that party scene. But one of the biggest things was that he started playing with his nose, snorting powder. It's crazy because I took my first toot of powder with Blaze. It was only after I had tooted with him a few times that Blaze told me how the shit wouldn't let him come up. I never let cocaine take over me. To be honest, I hated the high, and I didn't see what Blaze and the rest of the crew liked about it. I didn't want anything that would affect one, my money and, two, keep me from sleeping and eating. That cocaine did all the wrong shit for me, so cocaine for me was short-lived.

Within a year of hanging with Blaze, I had come up. Blaze had turned me on to a supplier that I called Unc. After a few months of dealing with Unc, he saw my potential. And what I had learned from being a student of the game before I started playing in it was that no one was going to help you or put you on unless they saw you trying to put yourself on. I learned that having a good face card in the streets will keep you afloat, but not depending on no one to give you anything will keep you ahead. You can't depend on anyone in the streets or the business world to help you maintain your business. It's on you to build relationships and have the right work ethic to take you to the next level in anything you do. By doing those things, I started to acquire things faster than the average hustler. At 17, I now had my own home and car and was moving a couple of ounces every couple of days. I was turning about eight thousand dollars a week. Before I knew it, I was supplying Blaze. During these days, if I wasn't with Blaze or my man, Flint, I was alone getting to it, chasing the paper with a vision of getting rich and becoming this legit businessman.

I became extremely serious about the vision when my first child, a baby boy named Keshawn, was born. He was maybe six months old when I got the news that I had a baby girl Branasia on the way as well. Becoming a father, honestly, made me go harder when it came to getting money in the streets. I really hadn't been stacking my money up, but with the birth of my two kids, I started to go hard. Getting out of the game to be this business owner and have my kids in a position to be whatever they wanted to be and never have to look towards the streets was my plan. When I got with my daughter's mom, Blaze didn't like it. He would always tell me that she wasn't the one for me. But by this time, I was rocking with her, and I didn't care what Blaze or anybody had to say; she was my lil rider. She had earned her spot. In the beginning, I never showed her anything that I had going on. I kinda played like I was down on my luck. At this time, my daughter's mom was living with her brother's ex-girlfriend in the project called The Drive that I used to hustle in back when I was in the tenth grade. She was cool with a guy's girlfriend who owed me some money for some weed that I had given him on consignment a while back. He had now come up a little bit and was doing good with the weed, from what she was telling me. She told me she knew where he was hiding his weed in his girl's apartment and said she could rob the whole stash if I wanted her to. So, of course, I sent her on the mission. I took her to the projects that morning, and like clockwork, when we pulled up to her home girl's apartment, she walked right in like she was home. After about 15 minutes of being in the apartment, she walked back out with a book bag and hopped in my car, and we pulled out just as smoothly as we rode in. She handed me the bag once we pulled off, and when I opened the bag, it had about two or three pounds of weed in it. At that point, I was fucking with her, but I could never fully trust her.

As she and I got close, me and Blaze started to stop

hanging as much. He started hanging with one of our other homeboys from Chap because I wasn't around as much anymore. Hanging with that homeboy would cost Blaze his life about six months before my brother's release from prison. The sad thing is that the night Blaze lost his life, we were all chilling at my uncle's pool hall. I pulled up that Sunday night, and Blaze was already there with our other homeboy. I backed in right in front of the pool hall, and Blaze came over. He told me that he was about to ride to the Ellison Club with our homeboy and another partner of ours named Guns. I told him that was bullshit because I couldn't get into that club because I wasn't 21. He talked a lil shit to me and then told me to let him get some of the Hydro weed I had just got in so they could smoke on the way to the club. I talked my shit to him about already owing me for some work I had given him. He talked a lil shit and told me he would pay me for everything that next day. He got out of my car and walked to the car with our other homeboy. When they crunk the car up, I jumped out of my car and yelled for my homeboy Guns, who had got in the car with them, "Yo Guns, man fuck them. Come roll with me, and let's blow on this Hydro I just got in." He opened the car door and got out of the car with Blaze and our other homeboy and told them he wasn't going to leave me in the hood by myself. That night, I would be Guns' angel because that night, my homeboy Blaze would die leaving the club in a car accident with our other homeboy. That night would haunt me to this day. Blaze was like a brother to me. I learned so much from him. If there was one person I knew would jump in front of a bullet for me, it was Blaze. When I say I knew, it was because he had done so before.

Life continued after the death of my man Blaze, but it wasn't the same. I stayed to myself for a bit, and the only one who knew how Blaze's death really affected me was my oldest daughter's mom, whom I was with at the time. She really helped me through that, and I salute her to this day for that. By the time my brother got released from prison from doing his three-year bid, I had come up. I wasn't the same little brother he had left in the streets for Blaze to watch over. I was now leaving my mark in these streets. When my brother left to do his prison sentence and had Blaze show me the ropes to this street shit, Blaze and I would always talk about having a bank put up for my brother when he came home. Blaze always would say that's what real niggas do for their comrades. So, when my brother came home, sure enough, I had him a little something put away. I didn't want my brother to hop right back into the game selling crack because, with his name alone, I knew that the narcotic officers would be on his trail as soon as his feet hit freedom. So, with that in mind, I sat down with my bro and gave him the rundown on what I had going on and how I had come up. I told him I wasn't giving him any cocaine or crack because I knew the narcs would be on his line, but I did have five pounds of weed for him and a few thousand dollars.

See, I really looked forward to my brother and I taking over and doing things together, but what I didn't know was that my brother had lost that drive. He wasn't the hustler he was before he left. Losing Blaze had really done something to him. The conversation really didn't go as I thought it would. My brother really wasn't picking up what I was putting down to him, and after that, my brother and I would hardly do any business together. If you have ever looked at the movie *American Gangster,* it is a scene in the movie when Frank Lucas was about to go to war with the crooked cops who had raided his house and taken his money. His mother demanded to speak with him before he left, and he stopped to hear her out. She looked at Frank and told him that when he called down south and asked all of them to come up north to New York with him, everyone stopped what they were doing, packed up, and left their life down in the South to come to do what it was he needed for them to do. She then looked at him and said, they all came, he called, and they all came running. She looked at Frank and said if he had been a doctor or lawyer, his brothers would have been a doctor or a lawyer because they looked up to him. His nephews, brothers, and all. When I saw that movie for the first time, I felt that to my core. I really looked up to my brother so much that had he been a doctor or lawyer, I would have been one, too. It really hurt that my brother and I would be so distant in the game because I chose this path following him. At this point, I was too far gone to turn back, or at least I thought I was.

Not even a month after my brother was home from prison would be when I caught my first felony drug offense. Just like I had thought, the narcs were on my brother, and I happened to get caught up showing my hand when it wasn't even my hand that the narcs were after. One morning around 11:00 a.m., I was lying on the couch at my mom's house when a horn was blowing outside. I was asleep and wasn't about to move to see who it was. Just so happened my daughter's mom was there with me, and the sound of the horn was aggravating her, so she went to the door to see who was blowing. She came back to the room where I was and told me that a lady wanted me. When I went to the door, it was the mother of an ex-girlfriend of mine who was from Chap. She asked where my brother was, and I told her I had no idea. Then she went on to ask me if I had anything. In my mind, she was looking for my brother, so she wanted weed because that's what I knew he was selling. So, I told her, "No, I don't have any weed." She then said she wanted some crack. It kind of threw me off, but I knew that she wasn't the police. I had known her for years, and she was like a play mother-in-law from the time I dated her daughter. So, I asked her what she wanted. She replied she was trying to spend twenty dollars, so I told her to hold on. I went back into the house and grabbed her a twenty-dollar piece of crack. I went back outside and went to the driver's door and handed it to her. She then pointed to the back seat and told me to get the money from the guy in the back seat. Up until this point, I thought she was alone. At this point, she told me it was him who had the money. She went on to tell me that she saw him riding a bike and asked her to take him to get something from Dirty, which is what the streets called my brother. See, just like I had felt, the narcs were going to try and get my brother. But anyway, I looked at her and back at him, and the whole thing just felt wrong. However, I had shown my hand to the wrong person this time because unbeknownst to her and me, as I would find out later, the guy she had picked up was wearing a camera with audio and video and was an informant for the narcs. My first charge ever would be conspiracy to conspire with my ex-girlfriend's mom to sell a twenty-dollar crack rock. With that charge, I really felt that there was no turning back at all. They had got me tangled up in the system. I was now all gas and no brakes. I was now a part of the justice system, or should I say, business.

4

UNKNOWN DANGERS

After the divorce of my parents, my life took a change for the worse. As a young man, I had no clue what it was that I was feeling. My dad still came around regularly, but it wasn't what I had been used to my whole life. His visitation days with us were Tuesdays, Thursdays, and every other weekend; he didn't miss one. He hardly got to see my brother because he was deep into the streets shortly after the divorce and hardly was home. So it was me who would be there for him to see. On these days, he would pick me up to take me somewhere with him, even if it wasn't anywhere but up to the local courthouse with him to pay his $300 weekly child support to my mom. He would let me see what he was paying my mom per week and explain what that money was for. He would tell me that the money he pays her is his part of the bills in the house we live in. He told me the money wasn't for my mom to give my bro and me like we had thought. He let me know that the money was for the bills, and the allowance

he gave my bro and me was for us to do as we like. When we needed shoes or whatever, he told us to come to him.

It would be on these days when my dad would also ride me around and talk to me about the streets. He would tell me things like, "Be careful when picking the guys you choose to hang around because birds of a feather flock together." He would say, "If you hang with people who use drugs, you will eventually use. If you hang with drug dealers, eventually, you will deal." He would say, "It's just life, Brandon." I remember on one of these rides, he would tell me, "The man selling drugs is more of an addict than the man using!" Now, for the life of me, I couldn't understand that statement my dad made. By this time, I was sneaking hustling just a little bit with whatever I could find in my brother's room, and it was no way that I was going to believe that I was addicted like the ones using drugs. As a kid, I really couldn't understand what he was saying, but what he was doing was trying to prepare me for the unknown dangers of the game. Really, from the outside looking in, you only see the allure of the game and not all the unforeseen and unknown dangers of the game.

By the time I was 17, I was full-fledged in the streets. I had learned a lot from watching the older guys that came up in the game before me, but there was a lot that I didn't know about the game as well. I remember early in the game, before I was full-fledged, one of the big homies in the hood from Chap named Noop had told me that he always kept his hand in another man's pocket so that he wouldn't have to be in the streets selling shit himself. He told me that he never sold hardly anything COD. He always fronted it out, but not enough to where it could hurt his re-up. Back then, I studied the big homie, and I noticed that he was really on top and staying low-key by dealing with his circle of guys he gave work to on consignment and keeping all the rest of the streets out of his business and unable to get close to him. I was close to him because his little brother and I were really tight coming up, and he gave us the game when we would listen. I took all this in when I was a teenager, so when I finally rose up to heights in my drug dealing days, it was the big homie's business model that I would use to keep me strong for as long as I was.

I also built myself a team of guys that I could give work to on consignment. Over time, I had my guys moving enough work per week on consignment that I had no room to deal with guys who wanted to do COD deals. This business model kept my chances low of making a direct sale to someone trying to set me up for the police and the chances low of me getting robbed during a deal. The model seemed perfect. I could move three or four kilos a week without losing sleep like other dealers I knew. To make the model work, I had to give good prices to my guys, even if it meant it cut into the profit I could have made had I sold it COD. I was cool making three to five thousand off a kilo, especially when it was weeks that I could move five keys and profit around $25k.

This model was cool until the local law enforcement couldn't get me to slip up. They were extremely pissed because I wouldn't allow them to extort me for money and information like I had seen them do a few of the older hustlers I came in the game under so they became pissed to the point they called the federal government in for help to get me because they knew what I was doing but couldn't seem to get anyone to flip on me and help set me up. See, when you are dealing on what they call the state level, it's nothing to pay your way right out of the simple cases they can get you on with the right attorney. The serious cases on a state level that you don't want to have to fight in court are trafficking, murder, and serious crimes. On a state level, you basically have to get caught with all the drugs or sell a lot to someone working undercover for the local law enforcement, at least that's what I thought. I was in the position to pay off the local law enforcement, and they never got one cent out of my hand nor a conversation because I had a great lawyer on retainer who worked with the sheriff and the chief sheriff and could have charges swept under the rug for me and my guys. See, to an 18-year-old kid with a foggy mind and a big bag of money, he had it made, but on the flip side of the allure of the game that I thought I had figured out was the unknown danger. What I didn't know was when you make money, and people get wind of it, people try to climb the ranks by coming for the one they think is on top. They come from all angles. You got cops who want to bring you down for a promotion. You got other dealers who want to come up the ranks by testing your gangsta and trying to make you look weak in the streets, and you got the robbers who want to be the ones to get the big fish.

See, the street life is full of stressful days and sleepless nights when you are dealing on a major level. It's not an easy job to sell a product that you can't advertise to the public for many reasons - a product that you have to try and sell secretly. You got several fast-food restaurants on every corner together who get to put up big signs with deals for the week, and some of them still struggle to make money. Fast food restaurants go out of business in America every day. So, imagine trying to make a million dollars off a product that you have to sell secretly for the sake of your life and freedom. So many dealers just like myself had a business model that worked and were able to see some real money out of the streets, but what we didn't have was knowledge of the unknown dangers.

See, the federal government launched the war on drugs in 1971. It was President Richard Nixon who signed it into law. And it was upheld throughout the Bush Administration and all presidents that followed up until President Obama shed light on these racist and biased laws and pushed for change during his time in office. The war on drugs, in reality, was a war on us, meaning the Black and the brown man. There were so many different sentencing schemes targeted to give the Black and brown guys long prison sentences for nonviolent drug offenses, even if they had never been in trouble before. They had laws in place to give you a life sentence for a first-time offense in federal prison for the sale of crack cocaine. See, what I didn't know, like many others that chose the path of hustling, was that the war on drugs was tough laws to incarcerate us (Black/brown) people, mainly the men, and break up our families. Leaving single mothers to raise the children on their own. Another thing is, in the United States Constitution, the 13th Amendment states that "Neither slavery nor involuntary servitude, except as a punishment for crime whereof the party shall have been duly convicted, shall exist within the United States, or any place subject to their jurisdiction!" meaning slavery was never fully abolished. It was transitioned to the form of prisons. So now it went from slave master to warden or CO. Never in a million years would I think I could go to jail for life without killing someone. Never in a million years did I think I could get 20 years in prison for just talking about drugs on the phone or knowing that a friend or associate was dealing and not reporting it to the law. It was possible because that conviction allowed the government to enslave the convicted. See, on a state level, as long as you don't get caught with the drugs, it's really nothing they can do, but when they make the call to the feds or your name ends up on a federal agent's hit list, it's a different ball game.

See, when I was arrested by the feds, I really thought that they were just wasting their time with me. When you think of the feds, you would think they would be after the drug lords smuggling drugs into the United States. What I didn't know was that the feds could indict a ham sandwich if they wanted to, which is a fact. See, during this war on drugs, the federal government created laws inside of laws that were intended and were used to give out enormous sentences to the Black and brown race. To be clear, I will only speak on my case, but many were entrapped into long prison sentences by the feds for nonviolent drug offenses, and many of these people being addicts and not even drug dealers. There are so many guys that sell drugs just to support their own drug habits. They see it as a way to satisfy their habit without having to steal, rob, or kill to get it. I know because I had some guys around me who would make sales for me just to support their habits.

During the local law enforcement's investigation of my drug operation, they were told by a confidential informant that I was selling large quantities of crack cocaine. So in January 2007, they wired that informant up and sent her out to buy crack cocaine from me. On the first buy of the operation, the informant got scared that the wire would be detected by one of my guys or me during the deal, so she took the wire off before pulling up to the spot to buy the drugs. When the informant drove up to buy the drugs, I sensed a feeling that something wasn't right, so I never spoke to her, and I gave the drugs to one of the smokers that we kept around so that he could do the deal with her for me. After that deal, I told my guys something wasn't right with her, and nobody should serve her again. Her body language told it all; my gut would not let me overlook it. After that day, the informant called me almost every other day, asking to buy crack, but I always told her I was not around or that I didn't have anything. Now, the local law enforcement was furious because I wasn't biting the bait, and the one time that I had, the informant had taken the wire off, so there was no proof that I sold her anything.

Now this is where the game gets tricky, and there is no way for you to see the danger of the crookedness of the law when they want you. What happened next was the local narcotic cops, along with the NC State Bureau of Investigation, started to send this informant to other drug dealers around the city to make drug buys. Some of these dealers I hung around, some I knew of but didn't deal with, and some I didn't even know. After each buy from these dealers, the informant would end the conversation by saying, "Talk to you later, Lil B," which was my nickname in the streets. They had this informant go around the city and buy drugs until she had brought enough to trigger a 10-year mandatory minimum sentence in federal prison if they could get the federal government to take the case and convict me. The amount that would trigger that was 50 grams. Not even two ounces, or should I say a street value of $2,500, but if convicted, you could be sentenced to between 10 years and life in prison. During these buys by the informant, she got one of the guys close to me to sell her half of an ounce while she was wired up. What the state did next was, in March 2007, indict me and two of my childhood friends on charges of conspiracy to sell 50 grams or more of cocaine base crack.

I kept a lawyer on retainer during my days of selling drugs, so when the indictment came down and they issued an arrest warrant for our arrest, I was notified by the attorney, and he arranged for me and my co-defendants to turn ourselves in. When we turned ourselves in, that is when we learned that the State Bureau of Investigations was leading the case. During the arrest, the state agent over the case introduced herself to me and told me that if I cooperated with her to bring down someone else, this case could be wiped away, but if I didn't cooperate, she wouldn't stop until this case went federal. I simply looked at her and told her, "Do what you have to do because I haven't done anything, and I'm not cooperating with anybody." We made bond instantly and, after about a week or two, met with my lawyer to go over the motion of discovery, which was all the evidence the state had against us. Once we went over it, we noticed that I wasn't on any of the voice recordings. My homeboy Ant was only on the recording because the informant had pulled up on him asking where I was, and he told her I was probably at my house that I had in the hood at the time. That was all he said on the wire. Now, my other co-defendant was on the wire selling the informant a half ounce, but there was no way for this state charge of conspiracy to stick on us. None of my co-defendants had a criminal record. Out of the three of us, I was the only one with a prior drug offense and I only had one from when I was 17 yrs old. Now, I did have another prior state conviction for assault, stemming from a fight I was in when I was 17, but other than that, I didn't have an extensive criminal record. All my other charges had been dismissed or dropped down to misdemeanors. After a few months of going back and forth to court for these charges, my lawyer got the cases dismissed in March 2007. Knowing I just dodged a bullet, my lawyer advised me that the feds could come and pick this case up and re-indict us at any time. He advised me that my co-defendants and I shouldn't get into any more trouble and we should be okay.

See, when my lawyer got to telling me about these federal charges and their mandatory minimum sentences, I started to realize these unknown dangers. I started to think about everybody I had sold the allure of the game to. I was understanding that I didn't know all there was to know about the game. There were some unknown dangers that I couldn't prepare myself for. See, I had been through everything I thought I could have been through in the game. I had seen murder, been a part of robberies, and wiggled my way out of the charges. It wasn't that I was better than the next guy in the streets; I was just prepared. I always looked at the flip side of a situation so that I could be prepared if the plan went another way. I worked in second nature that way, and it always paid off.

One example was when one of my sources that supplied me, tried to set me up. I had been dealing with this source for a year or two. Within that year or two, I learned a lot from this source. Not only how things worked on the next level of the game but also how legit business worked and how, in some aspects, it was symbolic of being a dealer. I had built a relationship with this source to the point that I would use my muscle to protect him in any way. But just like it says in the book *48 Laws of Power*, one of the laws states never outshine the master. In my case, make them feel as if you don't need them anymore. A few things that had transpired between my source and I had my spider senses up. So, I started to cross my Ts and dot my Is when dealing with him. With this particular source, I would get two or three keys per week, and we would meet at a predetermined location every Sunday night after midnight. This routine had been in place for a strong year, and not one time did we stray away from this routine. I never did any of the trafficking, but I had a few loyal females that handled this trip from the beginning. However, my phone rang on a Thursday, and my source told me he had three keys lying around the house and needed me to grab them because he was about to hop on a flight to LA to work on an album with an artist and didn't want to leave them at the crib. I reminded him that I still had a kilo and a half left from the

Sunday drop, but I would call my girl to see if she was in place to make the trip and grab that up for him. I made a call to my girl, and she answered and told me she was in Atlanta and couldn't grab it up til the next day. I told her cool and reached back out to my source and told him what I came up with, but he was persistent in me getting the work. So much so that he asked me to come get it myself. Now, since I had been doing business with him, it was only one time that I ever trafficked drugs back, and that was the first time I ever did business with him, and I made it clear to him that I wouldn't be the one doing the runs from that point on. His persistence is what threw a red flag at me. Since we had been doing business, no one other than my particular female had done this run. On top of that, it had always been on Sunday, and it was never me doing the trafficking. It was that feeling that I always had gotten, that I just never overlooked, but I tried to ignore it for some reason this time.

I was in my car just riding, playing the conversation between me and my source in my head, and I just couldn't shake the feeling that he was on some fishy shit. The only reason I thought I was tripping is because the work he was sending would be on consignment and if it got knocked off, he couldn't get paid. I just couldn't see him wanting me out of the way that bad. As I was riding, I made a left to ride through my hood while I contemplated what was going on. As I was riding through the hood, I passed one of the drug houses called the Hotspot, where a few of my guys posted up every day. I see my right-hand man and his lil brother posted and flagging me down. I stopped to see what was up.

My right-hand man Jr asked me what I was about to do, and I replied, "Trying to figure a few things out; come roll with me." As he started walking towards the car, his lil brother asked to ride with us because there wasn't any money coming through the hood this early in the day. As they were getting in the car, a thought came to my head, and I asked Jr did his brother have a license, and he said yes. My thoughts were to get a rental car when we got to the city to pick the work up, and from there, instead of having my man brother drive it back, he could just take it to the other side of town to my uncle's house, and I would get it later. That way, I can throw off my source and my man lil brother, so he thinks I always drop it at my uncle's crib. So, they get in, and I hop on the highway headed toward the city.

The city was about an hour away from where we stayed. Neither my right-hand man nor his little brother knew what I was on at the moment. As we started riding, Jr asked if some of the guys we fronted work to in the neighboring county of Anson were ready to re-up or something since we were heading in that direction, and I told him no. Then he looked at me and asked if I had run through the three keys we just got Sunday, and I told him almost. After all the questions from my man, I opened up and told him what was going on and how my source had been blowing me up to get these three kilos before he left for LA, but I also told him that I didn't feel right because none of this was normal. So, I told him the plan to grab the work and take it to the other side of town to my uncle's house and double back and get it when my girl got back in town, and he was cool with it.

See, my right-hand man knew the routine. Most of the time, It would be him to oversee the run and make sure everything went right when I couldn't be there. So, all this was normal to him, but he didn't seem to think anything was strange when I broke down what I was feeling. So just as planned, when we got to the city, I dropped Jr and his lil brother off at the Arab rental car spot that we always used since the early 2000s. I told them to go meet the source at the normal spot, get the work, call me, and I would send them the address to my uncle's house when they were heading there. I left the rental car spot and headed towards the west side to go see my son while I was in the city. But on the way there, something just kept telling me to go to the meet spot to look this guy in the face to see if I still got that vibe I had since he called me earlier that morning. So, I turned around and headed to the spot where the work was being passed off. When I pulled up, they had already made the pass, and Jr had just put the bag in the rental and was headed inside the restaurant. So, I pulled up and hopped out of my car and into the passenger seat of my source car. As I got in, he started telling me that he only gave my man one kilo and not three because one of his guys had just sold two. The shit just didn't sit well with me. If he sold two, he could have sold three or kept the last one at least. Why did he want me to have it? This whole thing was out of the norm. Even the car he pulled up in was out of the normal, and when I asked him about the car, he said it was a rental he had got for one of his workers. The source told me that he was on his way to the airport and that he would see me and tally up the score when he got back next week. I dapped him

up and hopped out of the car feeling the same way I did when I got in. Like this nigga was up to something.

After getting out of the car, I went into the restaurant with Jr and his lil brother. Before I could sit down good, Jr started telling me that it was only one and that we should just take this lil shit back instead of all the precautions I was trying to put in place. My response to him was, "Who's gonna drive it back?" because I wasn't. Jr looked at me and then at his brother and said, "Lil bro said he would do it. I told him we pay $500 per brick for the run." I looked at his lil brother and asked if he was cool with that, and he said, "Yea, just let me stop and get a pack of cigarettes." I said, "Cool," and we got up to make our move. Once outside, Jr went to get in the car with his lil brother and ride back with him, but for some reason, I told Jr to let him ride alone. Once on the road, Jr and I tailed the rental car through the city and all the way back to the country. Once we made it back into town, I went out around the rental car for the last leg of the run. Once, I went around the rental being driven by Jr's lil brother, we rode for like a mile or two when we noticed a sheriff K9 car sitting on the side of the road. From there, we made the call back to Jr's lil brother, who was about four car lengths behind us, to tell him to turn off into my man, Unc's yard, who lived right off the highway where we were at. The lil brother had already passed the house where we wanted him to turn, and he was now on the bridge that brought you into the county and couldn't turn around. Once off the bridge, the K9 car pulls over Jr's lil bro while we are still on the phone with him. The officer comes to the car, and we hear the officer ask him for his license and registration and tell him to sit tight. After maybe five minutes of sitting on the phone with Jr's lil brother, he tells us that the narcotics officer, Officer Andy, had pulled up on the scene. While we are still on the phone, we hear the narcotic officer, Officer Andy, walk up to the car and tell Jr's lil brother that he got there sooner than what they had assumed. He then asked him if he had anything in the car that he needed to tell them about. Jr's brother then tells them that he doesn't have anything. They then tell him to step out of the car so they can search it. Once outside the car, Jr's brother tells us that they just got the bag out of the back seat that had the kilo in it. Once they opened the bag, we heard the officers tell Jr's lil brother to take the drugs where he was supposed to take them to. Jr's brother tells the officer that he can't take it where it is supposed to go and that he didn't know it was there. At that point, I hung my phone up. Just like I had felt from the time I received that call that morning that something wasn't right about that call. It was me that the setup was for.

When it happened, me and my right-hand man turned around and headed back to the city to try and wrap our minds around what had just happened. I called my source to let him know, and I told him I was back in the city trying to figure out my next move. What happened next instantly let me know that it was him who had set us up. When I told him I was back in the city, he told me to meet him at our normal hangout, Uptown Cabaret. When we got there, he was now driving his Benz and wasn't on a flight like he had been screaming all morning. I couldn't figure out, for the life of me, why he would want me out of the way. I was loyal to him, and I was also a young breadwinner, twenty-two years old, to be exact. Once we sat down to eat, I and Jr's nerves were torn apart, but my source was sitting across from us, unbothered. He asked Jr if his brother was solid. Jr's response was, "I don't know what no man will do under that pressure. Brother or not, I can't say." After that, he started talking about how much money we had made in the last year and how much I should be sitting on. This conversation was really blowing me. I knew that this coward had done this to me, but at the moment, I was still in doubt. My main concern was I had a teenage kid caught up in the unknown dangers of my life. When you live this thing called street life, there are no rules to it. It's not always the guy you're selling to trying to set you up; it also can be the one you trust the most, which is your supplier who wants you out of the way. Being loyal to the wrong people can cost you your life or freedom. Either way, it equals you being put away and other people around being put in compromising situations that eat you up inside because, deep down inside, you know it's your fault that they're in the situation they are in.

See, you can't have integrity in the game. The man with integrity is the target. He's outnumbered by the vultures. See, I was starting to see I couldn't be who I naturally was if I wanted to continue in the game. When the integrity of the game is compromised, then the game can't be won. It's just an allure that makes you think the dealers are winning. The material things make us feel on top, but in all actuality, no one can truly win. In some way, shape, or form, you have to sacrifice someone else to get to the top, and even still, you can't truly win. A lot of folks may say it's the game and that you have to accept what comes with it. To live with that motto, you have to have a cold heart. See, my heart was cold to a point, but at some point, I realized that wasn't who I was. I had a heart, and over the past couple of years, not only had my right-hand's lil brother become a victim of my life of crime, but I had also lost my best friend when some guys robbed him but ended up killing him over some drugs that I had given him on consignment. At this point, I wanted out. I wanted better for myself and the ones around me who I had introduced to this game. The unknown danger was starting to wake me up, and the fog was beginning to clear,

CHAPTER
5

LOYALTY TO THE GAME

After this close call, I decided to enroll in the local community college to get my Associate's in business. I was starting to feel the walls closing in on me, and I knew I didn't want my story to end this way. Since I was a kid, I hated to lose, so I started focusing on doing something different. I was a hustler and could sell water to a well, so I knew I wanted to go into the business of selling something, but I just didn't know what business I would end up in. For the rest of 2007, I did a lot of research on buying into different franchises. I had already bought a few properties. I had a late-night liquor house in my hood that was doing around $4K a week. I started doing a lot of partying and getting next to a lot of party promoters and rappers trying to jump-start my entertainment company called 80'z Baby'z Ent. I had no clue as to what I was doing, but what I knew to do, like I had all my life, was to get next to somebody that was doing what I was trying to do and soak up all the game until I had enough to

take off on my own. I started getting close to a lot of rappers and managers in the music world because, in my mind, I had to get away from the drug game because the federal scare had me starting to look at the game differently.

I was still dabbling in the drug game, but nowhere near how I was before things got hot for me and my crew. I was really trying to push my way into the entertainment business. One of the sources I dealt with prior was in the music industry, and I became a student of how he handled business while our relationship lasted. He was responsible for some major artists' careers. While doing business with him, my goal was to learn about the entertainment business, so I got him to show me how to promote a party and step up to newly opened club owners and negotiate deals to use their establishment to throw a party. He gave me the game on starting my own LLC (Limited Liability Corporation) to make my company legit. When I got the game on how to make the company legit, I went to my two childhood friends, Ant and Jr, who were getting money with me at the time, and I asked if they wanted to go in on the company together. We came up with the name together, but when it was time to sit down and make it official, they both weren't ready, so I did as I set out to do, and I started my own LLC. I then started frequenting nightclubs where artists I wanted to work with would perform.

A few years prior, I had gone out with my brother to this club in South Carolina. The line was wrapped around the building. My brother told me and my crew to follow him to the front of the line. When we got to the front of the line, my brother called for the club owner. When he walked over, my brother handed him an attorney business card that his lawyer had given him earlier that day when he went to court. My brother told the club owner that he was Attorney Mr. Dean and that he had some family members in town and wanted to show them a good time and told the club owner to allow us to skip the line and enter for free and that if he ever needed any attorney assistance don't hesitate to give him a call. The club owner let us all in with no questions. From that day forward, I could finesse almost any club owner or security to get through the door with some VIP love. So, when I started hitting the clubs on my mission, it was nothing to get next to the club owner or the security guards that could get me close to the artist so that I could give them my business card and see if they were willing to work with a young CEO. Mostly, all that I approached were ready to work, and a few even stayed in touch with me. I was never a groupie, and I approached each situation as a business move. It wasn't about shits and giggles. I had business conversations with some known artists at that time. And if I didn't have a relationship with the artist, I did with their manager.

My encounter with one of my favorite rappers of all time from Yonkers New York is what gave me the confidence that I could be an entrepreneur in this legit business world. I actually met him by accident one night in a club in Fayetteville, NC. He had just beat a gun case in NC and had got booked for a walk-through that night at a club I happened to be attending. It would be my right-hand man, Jr, who would actually get me in the space with him for the introduction. We hit it right off, and I could tell in a matter of minutes while talking to him and his crew that these were some authentic guys and down to earth, just like my crew. I really could relate to them. By the end of the night, he got on the mic in the club and screamed that he had a little brother in the building, and that's where our relationship was born. He was the artist I discussed my first legit business deal with. During this conversation, I would learn what an artist's contract consisted of and also what a rider was. He and I would exchange numbers and remain in contact until the feds arrested me in September 2008. Through him, I would meet his friend and business partner during one of his store openings in Myrtle Beach, SC, that he invited me to. His friend and business partner and I would discuss opening a store in my city to sell up north merchandise like CDs and clothing. He would later introduce me to another well-known artist and his manager at the time in Greensboro, NC. He and I would discuss him performing at a show that I was planning on promoting later that year, and he gave me a great deal on the show price, and from that night, I knew I could be a successful businessman if I put the energy into it. I was being accepted by some well-known artists, and I knew that if I put the same energy that I put into the drugs into entrepreneurship, there was no way I couldn't win in the business world.

Around this time, I was in search of another avenue to get money, and it seemed as if every artist that I got next to was ready to work. Rick Ross even let my right-hand man Jr perform on stage with him and his artist Gunplay during one of their shows in Fayetteville, NC. See, I was in a position to take off with the entertainment business. I had capital, but

I wanted to take my homeboys to the top with me but they wasn't ready. I wanted to do and still be there for my guys. See, it couldn't be one foot in and one foot out for me because I was honestly loyal to my guys and this life we had chosen.

That's why when any of my guys went to jail, I posted bonds. I'm talking about $20K cash bonds, and I never looked for a penny back from my guys. See, when it came to the drug game and the guys I let get close to me, I approached every business deal as if I were the guy trying to come up on the other side of the table. See, it's been me vs. me. So, it was always like I was doing a business deal with myself. I wouldn't offer my guys something that I wouldn't take myself. I wouldn't try to pay my guy to do something I hadn't ever done myself and knew it could be done without a problem. So, instead of leaving my guys in jail or complaining about why they hadn't been stacking money like I did, I just tossed them another bag on consignment, and we got back to it. I've always lived by the motto, "Blood only makes us related, but love and loyalty make us family." When it came to my crew that was around me every day, I was willing to stand front line with them through any situation because I looked at them like family.

When I was ready to walk away from the game, I sat down with my guys and told them the plan. But none of my guys were at a place where they could walk away. My guys were my brothers, and the loyalty I had for my brothers wouldn't let me walk away and leave them behind. One of the old heads in Chap, named Blackcat, called me General Patton one day. As a 20-year-old kid, I didn't know who in the hell General

Patton was, so I asked, "Why the hell you call me that?" He said, "Man, you don't know who General Patton was? General Patton was the Army General known for standing front line with his soldiers and never sending them into any territory he wouldn't go into himself." He went on to tell me about how he watched me and my crew plot on drug territory for a day and come back the next day and take over the territory. He said that the way I moved with my guys was like General Patton when he led his troops with an iron fist. I didn't really understand why the old head saw me in the same light as General Patton, but however, all I knew was that my guys were my brothers. I wanted for them as I wanted for myself, and that was to use the game to get ahead and make a move in a positive direction. I never wanted to be a drug dealer for the rest of my life.

I called myself leaving the drug game in October 2006 after my right-hand man's lil brother got caught with a brick of mine. Only two people could have set him up, either my plug or my right-hand man, because they were the only two who knew what the young man was driving when he was pulled over with the kilo in the car. The funny thing is that the officer told the young man once he was stopped that he had gotten to the checkpoint earlier than expected, which let us know that someone had set us up. After the setup, I wasn't in the mental space to continue in the drug game.

For the first time in over ten years of me selling drugs, I was at a point in my life where I didn't know who I could trust, which was new to me. Since I had begun hustling at the age of maybe 13, I was around some loyal old heads from my hood in Chap, and they taught me to stand on being loyal and staying solid. When I was around 12, I started stealing crack from my brother. It would be these smokers in the hood who I trusted to let know I had crack for sale. One in particular that I let know was a smoker who was like family to us named Star. Star was the first person I ever gave crack to on consignment. You would think with him being a smoker that I wouldn't get paid for the drugs I gave him, but that wasn't the case. I remember my brother going out of town for a week and me rambling in his room and finding his stash full of crack. I remember giving Star five rocks at a time, and he would bring me back $80 off each pack I gave him. Before I knew it, Star had made me over a thousand dollars before the night was out. At this time, I didn't know anything about weighing drugs. So, when my brother got back in town, he was furious about who had taken an ounce of crack from his stash. I was so young at the time that he didn't suspect me of stealing it, but somehow, someone had told him that Star had been selling the same crack my brother had while he was gone. My brother and his right-hand man, Blaze, went and found Star and brought him back to my mom's house to confront him about it. No matter what they did to him or what they had threatened to do to him, he would not tell them how he had gotten the dope. He just kept telling them that he didn't know what they were talking about. That night, Star would have taken a bullet and still not told that I had given him that dope. That loyalty was the type of loyalty that was instilled in me from the time I began in the drug game. The problem was that days were now long gone, just like those old heads who instilled loyalty into me. Loyalty in the game was long gone, as well. I was so busy trying to be General Patton and stay loyal to the guys around me, who I considered my brothers, to the point I was willing to sacrifice my freedom so they could stay free.

In 2004, I took a felony charge of assault with a deadly weapon for my twin cousin, a charge ten years later the feds would use to label me a career offender and give me 188 months in federal prison based in part on that prior state conviction from 2004. It's very foggy living in the streets. I couldn't see that those days were long gone. I didn't notice that every one of those old heads who had instilled that loyalty to the game in me had all died in the game, got a life sentence from the game, died in prison, or got out only when their health forced them out. See, those guys who were loyal to the game had got taken out of the game, and these new guys with new game had started playing it differently. They say the game hasn't changed; it's just the players in it. But the game had changed. Nevertheless, I was still in the fog. So, when my brothers came running to me to get back in the game with them a few months later, I gave in.

In late December 2006, instead of pursuing the entertainment move like I wanted to, I hopped back in the game to help my brother out. That would be the worst decision I made in my life, but not one that I would regret. In January 2007, the NCSBI started their investigation into my drug operation. It would be March 2007 when the investigation ended. In hindsight, it all goes back to the car rides back in the day with my pops and the talks we used to have where he used to try and discourage me from selling drugs by telling me that the man selling drugs was just as addicted to the drugs as the person using them. In my case, even though I saw the game about to swallow me up and I had a chance to walk away while ahead, my addiction to the game and my loyalty to it made me stay when I knew I should have walked away. Looking at it from a different light, the game really hadn't changed, other than somewhere down the road, the rules got taken out, removing the integrity in it. Fast forward to today, we all must be loyal to something in life, but with that loyalty comes rules and boundaries. Also, mutual respect. Those are the things that you can have in normal life but not in the game.

CHAPTER

6

LET THE FOG CLEAR-
FINDING YOURSELF

The fog began to clear almost six months before the feds issued an indictment for my arrest. I was going to state court on a trafficking charge stemming from an illegal search of my mother's property. My long-time retainer lawyer, Bob, had the case beat. He was tied in with the local sheriff's office just as much as all the attorneys were, but my lawyer had just a little more pull than the average lawyer. There were times that he would tell me he needed $10K or $20K to get rid of a case for me. One time in particular, he sat me down and told me he needed additional money to grease the palms of the chief sheriff of my town. I never paid the arrangement any mind. I had the bread, and I paid it, and life just kept moving on for me. Well, when I was fighting this particular case, my lawyer got some inside information that the district attorney was trying to give my case to the federal government. I will never forget that day in 2008. My lawyer, Bob, called me to his office and sat me down. He told me, "Brandon, I got some bad news. I spoke to an inside source in the prosecutor's office this morning, and they are not going to touch your state case. They are in talks with the United States Attorney's Office and asking them to prosecute you federally." I was in disbelief. I knew about the feds from a few legendary heavy hitters from my town that went there before. There were two in particular that I knew were millionaires from the drug game that went to federal prison and came back, and I had the opportunity to not only do business with them but also hear their story about their rise and fall in the drug game. Their names were Lou and LA. When they came home, I got the chance to hear their stories about how they went to fed and what their experiences were with that situation. But that was as much as I knew about how the federal system worked, and in my eyes, I was nowhere near the level they were on when the feds got them, so I didn't foresee this coming.

During this meeting with my lawyer, he warned me not to get caught up in anything else while we sat and waited for the feds to come down with their indictment. He went on to tell me how much he would charge me to handle my case when it went federal, and he also went on to explain the night and day laws the federal system had versus the state laws. It was totally different. He explained to me the government's mandatory drug sentencing scheme. He told me I would face a mandatory 10-year sentence for 50 grams or more of crack cocaine. He explained that the only way for me to get under that 10-year sentence was if I cooperated with the federal government as a witness, and he advised me not to do that. He told me that he and his team would work hard to get me those ten years if it came to it, but before I left, he also reminded me not to get caught up in anything else.

See, I didn't feel too bad about what was happening to me because deep down inside, I knew why it was happening. There had been a few crooked narc officers since way back when I was a student of the game and hadn't entered the game yet. One, in particular, was the chief of the force. I had known about him and the extortion game he would put down from my days of hanging around my older cousins when I was maybe 10 or 11 years old. I heard the stories about him extorting dealers, and when they wouldn't pay, he did things outside of the law to put them away in prison. Early in my hustling days, when I was maybe 17 or 18, I began doing business with Linda, an older mixed female in her 30s. She was a hustler, and I began to supply her and went on to make a lot of money together. Every spot she had was doing numbers, and the police never fucked with her. Eventually, she would let me in on the relationship that she had with the chief. They not only had a sexual relationship at some point where a child was in question, but she also had a free pass to sell drugs as long as she gave intel on some drug dealers from time to time and helped him retrieve stolen goods from around the county that the drug addicts would steal and pawn to dealers. See, the thing was, though, he could only protect her outside the city limits where the sheriff had jurisdiction. The problem was she had run into trouble with the city cops. A lady she had been selling drugs to had become an informant for the city police and was able to set Linda up on a few occasions, and every time, the chief would call in for a favor to get her out. Linda and I became extremely tight, and she kept me protected for a long time through my early drug dealing days. To be a successful entrepreneur, you have to have the best tools, and the best tool is information! Linda provided me with the information I needed to keep me safe from the authorities during my hustling days. I would have her call the chief before I would make certain moves like re-up and traffic drugs through the county. On several occasions, I would listen to the convo on speaker when she would ask him where he was, and he would tell her where they were working and who they were trying to bust. My whole team was safe because of my sweet Linda for a while. Whenever the chief would be on anybody who was getting work from me or who I was associated with, she would call me and tell me to have them shut their spot down before the narcs could get there or send their informant in there to make a buy.

Shit really hit the fan one day when the city cops turned this guy into an informant from my hood named Tic. He told them I was selling weight of cocaine and crack and that he could set me up. I had done business with Tic before but only small business because that's what type of businessman he was. All of a sudden, he called me to buy an eighth of a kilo of cocaine, and I instantly asked him where the hell he was getting the money from, and he told me he had a crackhead who just got a big settlement, and he owed him $5K. I told him to come holla at me. I only wanted to look him in the face because I knew something wasn't right about Tic. Later that afternoon, Tic pulled up across the street. I sent one of my guys outside to tell him I was coming, but before I could go out of the house to check his temperature, Linda pulled up and came into the house. She came right over to me and told me not to sell Tic anything. She told me that the city narcotics team and the county were laid down in the woods behind my house, watching me and waiting on me to make that sale, and they were going to take me down. I instantly went out the back door, hopped on my four-wheeler, took off through the woods, and left Tic without speaking to him about anything. Linda had once again come through for me in a major way, but on the flip side, it put her in a fucked up situation with the chief. See, the same city narcs that had gotten her were the same narcs that were laying in the woods behind my house watching me when Linda came to my house and told me it was a setup, but also the chief who had told her what they were doing was laying there watching his girl interfere with a bust that he was on. Now, the city cops were looking at him because they knew that Linda was his informant and she had ruined their bust. It was a crazy situation. That night, the chief called Linda and told her he wanted her at his office at 7:00 a.m. that next morning because he wanted her to put a wire on and come buy drugs from me. He gave her no option. So, that night, Linda called me crying and told me that the chief wanted her to come and buy drugs from me in the morning, and she didn't want to have to do it, but he was making her and throwing up all the things he had gotten her out of. She told me what time she was coming and told me not to sell her anything. Sure enough, the next morning at 9:00 a.m., Linda pulled up to my house and asked me to sell her a half ounce of crack. Being that I knew she had the wire on and that the chief was listening, I told her that I was done selling drugs and that I had given my life to God, and that she should try it because it was a lot less stressful. Linda left, took that wire back to the chief, and returned to my house maybe an hour later, and I gave her her daily ounce that she would sell and left. Linda would protect me all the way up until I went to prison on my state sentence for accessory after the fact of an armed robbery in 2004.

While I was away, I still stayed in contact with Linda up until she got indicted federally while I was away. It was the city cops that really were behind her going federal. See, the chief had semi-retired and handpicked the candidate that took his place. The heat was on the chief for years of cor-ruption. He had put his team together and was now pulling strings behind the scenes as if he wasn't doing anything. However, when the feds finally got their hands on Linda, it was mainly because they wanted information from her about the chief, which she refused to give them. See, when I came home, I no longer had Linda to protect me from the law. The chief was no longer in the seat, but his hand-picked team was there doing as they were told.

When I came home from prison, I got right back to the hustling, and without Linda to protect me, the new narc named Robbie jumped right on my line. Not even a month home, Robbie ran down on me while I was about to make a sale at the hotspot in my hood. I left my truck and struck out on foot. After a short chase, I got away from the narc. However, he did have my truck towed in and told everyone out there to tell me he had a warrant for my arrest. I quickly called the longtime lawyer I kept on retainer, Bob, and he told me to lay low the whole weekend and meet him at his office at 9:00 a.m. that Monday morning. That Monday morning, Bob called the sheriff's office and demanded that they give me back my car immediately if there wasn't a warrant for my arrest. Of course, there wasn't a warrant, so they returned my car to me that day. Bob did advise me to get out of my small town because the sheriff's department had it out for me. See, I didn't take Bob's advice because I was just coming home and beginning to have some major motion in the game. What I didn't know was that the players in the game that I had come up with had begun to change the plays in the game up. They were doing things differently and breaking the codes. I realized it a few days after my lawyer made them return my car back to me. It was an older cat who was once heavy in the streets. I had brought a few quarter kilos from him in the past, but I looked up to him as a youngster. His name was Rider because he was a motorcycle-riding joker.

But anyway, unbeknownst to me, Rider and the narc Robbie were good friends. Rider had fallen off over the past year that I was away, so being that I was having some motion when he reached out, I picked up. He asked me to have a meeting at his house. Rider started by asking what had happened at the hotspot when the police took my car. Questions he already knew the answers to. He went on to tell me how he and Robbie went back to middle school. He told me that when he was up in the drug game, and Robbie was going through his divorce, he helped Robbie pay for his attorney.

He went on to tell me that Robbie was cool. He told me to trust him and that we could make some money if I just came to sit down and holla at him. I told him I would be there around 5:00 p.m., and he said that was cool. I pulled up at 5:00 p.m. like I had told Rider. I pulled to the back, and like always, he let the garage door up, and I went into the house through the garage. When I went in, Rider was rolling up a blunt. He immediately started telling me again about how tight he and Robbie were. He told me that when he fell off, it was times when Robbie would take drugs off of people and not arrest them and would turn around and give them to him. Rider propositioned me to call one of my suppliers, preferably a Mexican, to bring me five kilos, let him know when they were coming and what they were driving, and Robbie would pull them over and take the drugs and tell them to get out the county. Robbie would then bring us the drugs, and we would have to give him a twenty percent cut on what we make.

Hearing this shit come out of Rider's mouth was fucking me up. I was a man who stood on morals and principles. I was always taught the code of the streets coming up as a youngster, so what Rider was pitching at me, I wasn't feeling at all. All I told him was I needed to think on it. As he was just finishing up the proposition, I saw the narc, Robbie, pulling up in his unmarked black car on Rider's surveillance monitor he had in his front room. Rider let the garage door up, and sure enough, while we were in Rider's house smoking a blunt, the narc, Robbie, came walking up into the house. He came in and spoke to Rider, and then looked at me and asked why did I call my lawyer and get him involved when he had my truck towed in. He told me that he had heard what I was driving, and he had seen me up to the hotspot and was really just stopping to holla at me to see how I was doing. He then looked at me and asked me if Rider had spoken to me about what he could do for us, and I said yes. He then handed me my phone that he had taken out of my car when they had it towed and told me just to let Rider know when I was ready. I took my phone from Robbie, and I left Rider's house, not believing what the fuck I had just witnessed. The crazy thing about the situation is that the whole circle of guys I used to get my supply of drugs from before I went to prison were now dealing with the narc. It wasn't just Rider. I ended up putting a target on my back when I refused to give up the morals and principles that were instilled in me by not jumping on board with the rest of the guys when it came to dealing with the narcs. I was one of the ones who refused to give them a cut of my take nor give the information on folks in the streets. Instead, I started to tell other dealers who I knew stood on the code not to deal with certain dealers, and instead, they started dealing with me. With the word starting to spread that I was telling people about what dealers were paying off the narc and giving them information, it started to affect a few of the dealers' pockets that were in competition with me, and they couldn't stand it. So, they started telling the narc that I was spreading the business in the streets, which gave the narc a hard-on for me. They wanted me off the streets more than anything.

At the time, I had a bar in my hood called the Do Drop In. One day, I was sitting out in the front of the bar with a few of my guys, and this narc, Robbie, and his partner, Bowe, pulled up in the yard. They both exited their unmarked jeep and approached me. I stood up and asked Robbie who they were looking for, and if they didn't have a warrant, I wanted them off my property, and I told them that I would be calling my attorney. Robbie got up into my face. He was beet red as he told me he had heard that I was running around telling people he was taking bribes. He told me that he wouldn't allow me to have him put under federal investigation and that before he went fed, I would go first! He looked me dead in the eyes and told me that I was his project and that he wouldn't stop until he had me sent to federal prison. I looked right back into his eyes and told him to get the off my property. He and his partner then turned around, returned to their unmarked jeep, and left. My guys, who were standing around and witnessed what had just happened, were in awe. My man POB was the only one who made a joke out of it, but Ant and PJ knew that the narcs meant everything that they had just said. A few months later, the narc, Robbie left the sheriff's office, but his partner Bowe, that was with him and witnessed the altercation between us, happened to move up to head narc due to the actual head narc taking a leave of absence. When Bowe got in the position, he called the SBI, the N.C State Bureau of Investigation, to have them open up an investigation into me. The way that he got them so enthused about investigating me was by telling them that I knew about some corrupt officers within the sheriff's department.

In September 2008, the U.S. government indicted and arrested me for conspiracy to sell 169 grams of cocaine base crack along with two of my childhood friends, Ant and POB. I was what you would call the head of this small conspiracy, meaning the target of the case. It was really a petty case. One hundred twelve grams of the amount they held me accountable for was from relevant conduct, a term the United States government uses when they want to enhance the seriousness of your instant offense by increasing the amount of drugs from which you actually got caught with and adding additional drugs to your account from which some stranger/ snitch said he bought or gave to you years prior. In my case, they added 112 grams to my drug weight from a prior charge I had in state court when the feds picked me up. However, I never was convicted for that state-prior charge. The charge was actually dismissed out of state court for lack of evidence. The feds still used the drug weight, calling it relevant conduct to my federal charge even though I caught my federal case a year later after that state charge had been dismissed. So, in actuality, it was only 57 grams of crack that the government informant brought, and 42 grams of that, the crooked narcotic agents over my case had their informant buy from another dealer in my hood named Big Head that I had nothing to do with. I would later find out that after the informant brought the drugs from Big Head because she was wearing a wire, she would say, "See you later, Lil B," as if she were buying the drugs from me, but in actuality, she was leaving Big Head's house. Big Head would later get indicted by the feds for an unrelated charge and would write a letter on my behalf to the federal prosecutor over my case and tell them I had nothing to do with the drugs that were bought at his house. In response to the letter Big Head wrote, the government would strike 28 grams from my drug weight but not the whole 42 grams that Big Head had told them I had nothing to do with, mainly because if they struck the whole 42 grams, then that would have taken my conspiracy from 50 grams or more, which carries a mandatory minimum of ten years in federal prison, to less than 50 grams which only carried a mandatory minimum of five years. For a while, I thought that Big Head had set me up because this government informant had gotten my number from him. Not only had Big Head given this informant my number, but it would also be Big Head's address in my paperwork stating that's where several drug buys took place that I supposedly orchestrated. In the motion of discovery from the government, not only was I orchestrating drug deals at this address, it was said that I drove cars that belonged to Big Head and his right-hand man, Big Boy, along with the tag numbers of the cars, all of which wasn't true. I was furious when I read this in the government's evidence.

I went right to the phone and called out to the streets, trying to get a couple of my people to get the tag numbers off Big Head's and his man Big Boy's cars to see if they matched the tag numbers on my paperwork. I knew the description of the cars matched what Big Head and his man big boy drove, but I wanted to really see if the tag numbers matched what was in my motion of discovery. To my surprise, when I asked a few of my people to get those tag numbers, it immediately had people in the streets questioning whether I had started cooperating with the feds. My own people, at that. In a sense, I can understand people who didn't know me thinking that way because they didn't know me; therefore, they didn't know the morals or integrity instilled in me. See, this hard-on that the sheriff's office had on me where they were willing to entrap me in this federal case began when I came home and got entangled with Linda.

I never cared about how somebody felt about me that I didn't deal with, but for the guys who were close to me to think that of me really caught me off guard. See, the people you don't care about can only obtain information about you from the ones you do care about. Don't let that go over your head. Anybody that was around me knew that my motto was that nothing beats the cross but the double cross. I've always been a man of integrity and a spiritually fearing man with the mentality to treat people how I want to be treated in return. That's why the only time I would ever cross a man is if he crossed me first because nothing beats the cross but the double cross, but you gotta always be looking for it. Not that you can stop it from happening because the cross normally comes from someone in your circle who's close to you, so, that being, you have to trust that person in some way, form, or fashion. Just the slightness of trust is all it takes for them to get close enough to put you in a cross, but if you are looking for it, like me, at all times, you can brace for it and sometimes pivot with the double cross. See, I always got my lick back, but I never put a man in the cross if he wasn't trying to harm me or stop my motion. All the people around me knew that about me. I couldn't believe the things I heard coming from the ones closest to me. It really hurt more than some physical pain. When I started hearing the things that were being said about me, I started to realize that this situation was about to clear up this foggy storm in my life.

See, this wasn't quite my first rodeo doing prison time. I had done eleven months in state prison, maybe five years prior, for accessory after the fact of an armed robbery. The case stemmed from a robbery that my brother and his friend committed. The robbery just happened to happen at the house of a smoker who had called me there to buy drugs. During what the police called a drug deal gone wrong, a Mexican man was shot in the head. From that experience during the time I had to fight the robbery case, I knew how pressure from facing time behind bars would make your own brother write an incriminating statement against you, so I didn't sweat it when the smoker whose house it happened at was taking the stand on me during my trial. From experience, I knew that the right pressure would make your right-hand man become a government witness against you, but I didn't know how your so-called friends would write you off and let their true feelings about you come out when they felt like you were finished. See, my indictment was small. Just me and two of my guys. But my circle was big because I would let anybody eat. I was that guy who tried to bring the city together and eat off one big plate. The thing was, nobody went down with me. No indictments came down on anyone associated with me other than my two original co-defendants in my case. Only the guys that were arrested with me really knew that the case we were facing was really petty. The only reason they wanted me so badly was because they really wanted me to cooperate with them to take down the sheriff's office in my town. See, the people in the streets knew me for moving kilos, so quite naturally, when the streets heard the feds arrested Lil B, they instantly went to thinking that there were heavy drugs involved. Unbeknownst to the streets, my case was really a petty federal drug case. The pressure was applied to me because I was a man of integrity while hustling in the streets from day one. See, when I first jumped off the porch into the life of crime in my little town, for the most part, the police had to do their job and solve cases. Now, don't get me wrong, there has always been some snitching in the streets going on, but it was rare. It was more undercover cop-shit back then.

See, once I jumped into this game, it was like there was instant fog blocking me from seeing a lot of things change right around me, and I did not realize it. I began to understand that I was caught in a matrix maybe one month before the feds served their indictment against me and my co-defendants. It would be one of the legendary hustlers from my city who had gone and spent a bunch of time in the feds back in the early 90s. His name was Rico. Rico was a known legend. A millionaire drug dealer that I had the opportunity to be blessed with some of his game when he was first released from federal prison. I would hang out with him, and he would tell me the stories of how a famous rapper from brooklyn New York would come and buy drugs from him and owed him fifty grand and how he went to prison with other famous rappers. He would tell me about him doing business with the founder of the Sex Money Murder Blood Gang, Pistol Pete. I really looked up to Rico. I had heard rumors that he had gotten a life sentence in federal prison but had come home in ten years.

Like I said, I hardly knew anything about the federal system. All I knew was that he had done a decade for drugs. He hadn't killed anyone, so in my mind, ten years was a long time for selling drugs. Rico called me out of the blue about a month before my indictment had been handed down. He said, "Hey, Sporty, are you home? Instinctively, I said yea. He then told me he was about to pull up and that he really needed to talk to me. His telling me he was pulling up threw me for a loop because Rico had never been to my personal home where I laid my head. So when I saw him pulling up on my surveillance camera, it baffled me. The sound of his voice on the other end of the phone led me to believe that whatever he wanted to talk to me about was important. I went outside and sat in the passenger seat of Rico's truck. Once inside, Rico began to tell me that he knew about the trouble that I was in and that he knew someone who could help me out of the trouble. He went on to tell me that he knew a federal agent who could help me out of the trouble I was in if I would be willing to tell the agent everything I knew about the corrupt cops within the sheriff's department. Preferably, the chief! He then opened up a briefcase and handed me a stack of papers. He told me it was his pre-sentencing report from his federal case from the 90s. He went on to tell me that he had the chief on the payroll all through his drug dealing years back then, paying him $5K a week for a pass to not only sell drugs but also protect him from any other authorities taking him down. He went on to tell me that the chief failed him when it came to protecting him, and in return, he cooperated with the federal agents against the chief. As I read Rico's pre-sentencing report, it was there in black and white on federal documents that Rico had worn a wire during several meetings that mostly occurred at Rico's home in his garage. Clear in black and white, I was reading how Rico had captured conversations between him and the chief discussing bribes. One of the recordings even captured the chief trying to give Rico drugs out of the evidence room at the sheriff's office.

After reading all the evidence that Rico had gotten for the federal government against the chief, all I could do was look at Rico and ask him, "Why was the chief still on the streets?" Rico looked at me and said the only thing he could think of was that the chief had some people in high places who were protecting him. I then looked at Rico and said, "What possibly could I tell them on this cop that you hadn't already told them?" He then went on to tell me that all I had to do was tell them anything that I knew or heard about the chief and that his agent would help me out of the trouble I was in. After sitting there for a few more minutes, I then told Rico that I had some things to do and that I would talk more with him later about that. He told me okay, and I exited his truck.

When I got back into my house, I sat on my couch in awe! Here was another living legend in my eyes who had just lost his stripes with me. Not only had I read what he told on the chief of police, but I also had seen in the report that he had cooperated with the federal government against the founder of the Sex Money Murder Blood Gang, Pistol Pete. At that very point, the fog was beginning to clear, and I was finally seeing the drug game for what it really was - a fucking trap! See, when it's good, everyone is around claiming they love you. It will even have you feeling like they will kill anybody who tries to harm you, but in actuality, it's all the allure of the game. When the heat comes down on you and the storm begins to tear down what you have built, you find yourself by yourself, and mostly everyone who was around, reaping the benefits of your hustle, will leave you to fight alone. When the fog began to clear, I realized I couldn't re-write a story that had already been written. I just had to suck it up and accept the role written for me in this story called life.

CHAPTER

7

ESCAPING THE ALLURE
OF THE GAME!

When I was indicted and arrested in 2008 by the U.S. federal government, I was never given a bond. I was betrayed by the judge. At my bail arrangement, the U.S. attorney determined me to be a flight risk due to the amount of time the government said I was facing. During the bail arraignment, they had me and my two co-defendants in the courtroom together. When we entered the court-room, for some reason, the U.S. Marshals began to split my co-defendants and me up. They sat me and my co-defendant, POB, at the table in front of the judge and my co-defendant, Ant, at a table off to the side with his attorney. As I sat at the table with my lawyer, listening to him explain his approach to getting me a bond, he told me it was always worth a try, but it normally only really happens if you were cooperating with the government, which I wasn't. Next to me was my co-defendant, POB's lawyer, and on the other side of him was POB. After my lawyer gave me the game plan, I sat back to relax and wait for the judge to enter the courtroom so we could get this show on the road. We had been in the Durham County Jail approximately one week before we got the bond hearing, and I had somewhat prepared myself for whatever I had in front of me.

For this first week, they had my co-defendants and me in the same jail block, so we had been plotting our strategy the whole week. We all took an oath between the three of us to stay ten toes down throughout this fight, and whoever happened to come home first or beat the case take care of each other's kids first, then hold one another down in jail. We all were family, brothers for real, so not for one moment did I feel like either one of them would fold because I would have died before I folded on my brothers. Our case was petty from the jump, and my lawyers said the same thing about the case. So, as I was relaxing, waiting for the hearing to begin after speaking with my attorney, I began to overhear POB's attorney, who was right next to me, saying, "Mr. POB, my plan is to waive your bond hearing today. I have already spoken to the U.S. attorney about this case, and they have informed me that their target on this case is Mr. Brandon sitting over there," and he looks over to the table across the courtroom where my co-defendant, Ant, and his attorney were sitting. I am all ears at this point. I looked at my attorney, who was sitting to my right, because I knew that he was hearing what I was hearing as well. POB's attorney went on to tell him that Mr. Brandon was the target and, that the U.S. attorney wanted him to cooperate with them on me, and that he could have him out in a few months. He went on to tell POB that if he didn't cooperate, he would probably get 20 years. I looked at my attorney, furious. He saw me about to explode and kinda gave me a look to remain calm and act like I hadn't heard anything. For some reason, POB's attorney thought that I was Ant, so he let the cat out of the bag, not knowing Mr. Brandon was sitting right beside him. All our families were sitting behind us in the courtroom, and after trying to hold in what I had just heard this lawyer say, I looked back and yelled out to our people to hire POB a lawyer because he was trying to get him to turn on me. The attorney immediately got the U.S. marshals to move him and POB to the table where Ant and his attorney were sitting. After about 15 minutes of sitting and waiting for the judge to enter, he came in and heard from our attorneys and the United States attorney. After a few minutes of acting like he was weighing the evidence from both sides, he denied all our bonds, and they sent us back to the Durham County Jail to await trial.

It was at this point in my life that I began to escape the allure of the game. I had begun to see a side of the game that no one talked about. The dark side of the game when the glitz and glamour are no more, and it's little old you versus the United States of America. I spent $30,000 for my defense team despite all the guys I talked to in the county jail telling me to save my money because there was nothing a hired attorney could do that a federal court-appointed lawyer wouldn't. It was hard for me to take that advice from them guys because I noticed most of them that had court-appointed attorneys were cooperating with the government to take other dealers off the streets, and I never intended to talk my way out of this situation I had gotten myself into. My thing was to pay my attorney to talk my way out of this just as they had in the past, or if not, get me the lowest sentence they could get me without me having to cooperate. After six months in the federal holding facilities, the government offered my first plea. It was an open plea, with a mandatory minimum of 20 years to life in federal prison. My instant offense carried a mandatory minimum of ten years, but due to what the government calls an 851 enhancement, which is a notice to the court that a defendant before them has a prior state drug conviction, which allows them to double the mandatory minimum and give you a stiffer sentence than what the instance offense calls for. Never in a million years would I have believed that our justice system would have such an unfair sentencing scheme. I refused to agree to sign a plea agreement with a mandatory minimum of 20 years. After about a month or so of arguing back and forth with my attorney and the U.S. attorney, the government agreed to drop the enhancement and offered me an open plea with a mandatory minimum of ten years to life in prison. I signed my plea and began to prepare for ten years in prison for a non-violent drug offense.

Prior to this federal case, the only other drug case on my state record was for the sale of a $20 crack rock when I was 16 years old. It was my first offense, so I didn't get any jail time, but I did receive six months of probation. Yet, the U.S. attorney was using the NC misdemeanor to portray me as a career drug offender. So, after I signed my plea agreement, I remained in the county jail waiting on what the government calls a pre-sentencing investigation (PSI) before I could go to court to be sentenced. The PSI was an investigation into your life prepared by a U.S. probation officer who gathers information for the judge and gives him a recommendation on how much time a defendant should be given. Another part of the federal sentencing scheme that was unfair to me. Why would the judge need a probation officer to recommend to him what sentence to give a defendant? At this point, I noticed that the judge's power was limited in federal court.

After waiting another six months, the probation officer finally made a recommendation on my case. She recommended that I receive between 262 months and 327 months. I instantly told my attorney I wanted to take back my plea agreement and go to trial because the same prior conviction the U.S. attorney agreed not to use for purposes of 851 enhancement in my case, the U.S. probation officer was using to enhance my sentence as a career offender. During the conversation with my lawyer, he reassured me that it was just a recommendation and the judge was not bound to it like he would have been bound by the 851 enhancement to give me 20 years had I signed the first plea. My defense team prepared the arguments for sentencing. On September 23, 2009, I stood before the U.S. judge, not knowing what was gonna happen with my life. My lawyers argued diligently that I shouldn't be sentenced as a career offender solely because my state's prior conviction for the sale of cocaine was not a serious drug offense, and at the time of the instant offense, I hadn't had a drug charge in almost ten years. Also, the instant offense would not carry anywhere near ten years had there not been the 100/1 crack-to-powder ratio in place from the biased/racist War on Drugs from over 30 years ago.

After hearing arguments from both sides, my attorney asked for a ten-year sentence, and the prosecutor recommended that I not be sentenced as a career offender but to a 20-year sentence under Section 4a1 of the federal sentencing guidelines. He stated on the record that normally, when he sees a career offender standing before him that he normally sees a prior record a mile long, but in my case, he didn't see that. So, the United States judge decided to sentence me in the middle to 188 months, which was 15 years and eight months. The courtroom was filled with my closest loved ones. At this point, I looked around at my family in the courtroom and saw my parents and children crying as if we were at my own funeral….and I was being buried alive! The allure of the game was no more. I was beginning to see life for what it really was at that moment, and at that point, I realized that what I did and how I lived my life affected not only me but also my loved ones. For so long, the allure of the game had me mesmerized, and I couldn't see that the game was just a facade.

After sentencing, I remained in the county jails for another few months. While I was waiting, I began to work out and get fit. It seemed like my stress reliever and a way for me to think without being bothered or interrupted. While waiting in the Hillsborough County Jail, I began talking to an older Black guy called Foote. Foote had been sentenced to 20 years three years prior and was now back on an appeal to fight his sentence. I began to take a liking to this old head named Foote. I told him I had just been sentenced to 188 months and that the U.S. prosecutor had withdrawn his section 851 enhancement. However, the U.S. probation officer used the same state prior to recommend that I be sentenced as a career offender. I just felt like that wasn't right. I knew I wasn't a career offender legally. When I began telling Foote about my situation, he started to open up to me. I told him how I felt like they were mad because I didn't tell them what they wanted to hear. Foote didn't say much on that, but he looked at me and said, "Youngin, don't you do nothing where you can't get up in the morning, look in the mirror, and feel like a real man about yourself." After letting it settle in my mind about what he said, for a quick second, I knew then that I must not let the situation take my integrity, which I had seen done to a lot of guys before me. However, Foote went on to tell me that he would write my direct appeal to appeal my sentence. Before writing my direct appeal, Foote made sure to tell me that if I was cooperating, he didn't want to help and that if I were, this appeal would upset the U.S. attorney and that he wouldn't recommend a time cut for substantial assistance under Rule 35b of the U.S. sentencing guidelines later down the road. I assured him that I wasn't waiting on a time cut for assistance, and he began to help me write my appeal.

After writing my appeal, Foote then told me why he was back in court. He told me how he had been fighting his sentence since he was sentenced around 2005. Foote had won his first appeal in the 4th Circuit Court of Appeals and was remanded to the district court for resentencing. However, his sentencing judge sentenced him back to the same sentence and shipped him back off to federal prison. Foote's argument was that his NC state prior conviction for possession with the intent to sell and deliver cocaine should not be used in federal court to enhance his federal sentence because it is not a serious drug offense in North Carolina unless you are a repeat offender. Foote began to tell me about different case laws that backed his argument and how this appeal process went. He told me to get right into the Law Library when I got to the prison yard because I had the same argument he had, which was grounds for resentencing. Being that I had read Foote's paperwork, I knew that what he was telling me was real. What baffled me was how the federal prosecutor would battle you to keep you in prison when clear as day, all the evidence is saying that you are over sentencing these guys. Before my sentencing, the President of the United States of America wrote a memo to all United States prosecutors directing them not to object to lighter sentencing for non-violent crack cocaine offenders because the 100 to 1 sentencing ratio compared to cocaine was racist and biased. Even with the President saying this publicly, it didn't stop the United States federal system from over sentencing mainly the Black and brown guys.

I began to take a step out of my body to really take a good look at this picture. At the end of October 2009, I was put on a federal inmate transport bus from the Hillsborough County Jail. I was driven with several other federal inmates, 95% Black or Hispanic, to the Raleigh/Durham Airport. At the terminal of one of the biggest airports in North Carolina, while regular citizens are boarding flights for normal life things, here I was, sitting on this bus shackled from hands to feet, watching as several other buses pull in, making a half-circle around this gigantic airplane. Once all the buses were there, which looked like maybe 20 different buses from different county and federal holding facilities throughout the middle and eastern districts of North Carolina, U.S. Marshals began exiting the planes and getting big assault rifles from underneath the plane. You then had Marshals making their way to each and every bus on the landing strip with a list in their hands, stepping on each bus and doing roll calls. I began to pay close attention to what seemed like business as usual for them, but in my mind, from the information I had begun to gather about the laws and private federal holding facilities, I knew that this was more than just a war on drugs. From hearing other inmates' cases and the time they were getting, I noticed that it wasn't just me who had gotten over-sentenced; it was all of us. The sad thing was that hardly any of the inmates were paying attention to what I was seeing. We had just become victims of legal slavery; at least, that's what it felt like. Something that our ancestors had fought so hard to do away with, but here we were in the 20th century, still going through. By no way was I innocent, but the sentence for me and so many others was unjust.

As I sat back, I saw how we were being ushered onto this plane like some high-dollar cattle after being almost strip searched right outside on this landing pad at one of the biggest airports in North Carolina, and everyone just going on like this was okay. Here I was, having been convicted of a crime in the state of North Carolina but being shuffled onto this plane in North Carolina and flown all the way across the country to Adelanto, California, to serve my time. When sitting and pondering on this, it didn't take a genius to know that this was some big government business going on. A lot of whys began to come into my mind, and I couldn't wait to get to where I was going to start doing my research on this big money scheme that I had fallen victim to. I had been tricked by the allure of the game because no one had told me about this part. After about five stops around the country at other major airports to let inmates off and onto the plane, we finally made it to Victorville F.C.I. before 6:00 p.m. west coast time. Like I said at the beginning of this book, from a child, I was very observant, which most called nosey. Today, I say being nosey, as they called it, kept me alive in the streets and through a 15-year prison sentence. Being observant throughout this whole flying process, I saw that the plane remained filled to capacity throughout this whole day of flying. How many inmates the marshals let off is the same amount that got on.

I just remember telling myself that this wasn't about the crimes we had committed for the most part; this was a big business that I had become a part of, and the dope boy web had been designed just this way to incarcerate us. As soon as we got to the Victorville F.C.I., I and about 29 other inmates were sent through what the B.O.P. calls the receiving process. I would be lying if I didn't say that I was a little scared of what I was about to endure, but I will say that I had done a lot of talking with God throughout this whole process, and I was determined to come out of this situation alive and better than I was before. My favorite rapper Jay-Z once said something like this on his first album, "Reasonable Doubt," in the song *Can I Live* that someone can lock your body, but they can't trap your mind, and I was heavy on not allowing this situation to break me mentally. Jay-Z's "Reasonable Doubt" album has always been my favorite album. I could rap almost every song word for word when I was 13. The thing was, I was just listening to it, but I wasn't hearing it. See, Jay was rapping about this business I was just being introduced to in the late 90s, and I was now starting to see life as he saw it as he rapped about on *Can I Live*. However, During this receiving process, you go through your initial physical and mental health screens and meet with unit managers and case managers whose caseload you will be on. It is also when you meet with the captain of the prison and the SIS lieutenant. These are the guys who ask you if you have cooperated with the government before they release you into the regular population. They give you fair warning to let them know right then so they can put you in solitary confinement so that no harm is done to you. Right then, another "why" light bulb went off. Why would they try to make every inmate flip and become a government witness, then throw them in jail where their life is at risk? Once again, all I could come up with was this is a big business. During one of my conversations with Foote, he told me never to accept or claim the time. He told me to fight til the end, and I was prepared to do it. See, the allure of the game doesn't allow you to see the whole playing field. It only allows you to see what's in front of you.

8

CHAINS BROKEN

After our screening in the receiving department, we were allowed to go to our designated dorms for the general population that night. Off the bus that I came in on, only three of us went into the dorm I was assigned to. Luckily, I was assigned to a cell with a guy from Florida who I had sat beside the whole airplane trip that day. When we walked into the dorm, one of the first things I noticed was how segregated the inmates were. Prior to this federal sentence, I had done an 11-month prison sentence in North Carolina before, and it looked nothing like what I had just walked into. As soon as I walked in, I noticed all the Blacks sitting off to the left in this dorm made from concrete that puts you in the mind of a warehouse. They were all sitting in the middle of the floor watching TV. To my right were, I guess, you can call them my other race group. There were the Asian Islanders who all shared one TV. Then, right next to them were the Sur 13 Mexican gang members; they had two TVs, and then across the dorm, directly in front of the Sur13 guys, was a Mexican group of Pisces. What I learned was that they were just regular Mexicans from different parts of Mexico, mostly waiting to get deported back to Mexico after doing their time for illegal entry into the U.S. A lot of them were caught with large quantities of cocaine, but their drug cases mostly would get thrown out, and they would plead to illegal re-entry in the U.S. and get a couple of years then return to Mexico.

See, no one was really paying attention to the small things, but I was. How in the world could these Mexican guys get caught smuggling drugs into the United States of America, and when they get caught, their drug charges get dismissed, and they plead to illegal entry and only get a few years? It didn't make sense to me how the only ones who were getting all the time for the pettiest crimes were the colored men. On the same side of the dorm beside the Pisces was your sprinkle of whites who only had one TV to watch together as well. Once I walked into the dorm, I stopped for a second at the door and scanned the room to see what I was walking into. After scanning the room, a few Black guys walked up to me and asked, "What's good, homie? Where are you from?" I quickly replied, "North Carolina." The guys then told me that I had one homeboy in the dorm from North Carolina and two from South Carolina. They called out to the guy from North Carolina, and he instantly came down to introduce himself. He told me his name was Rock, and he was from Fayetteville, North Carolina. I instantly felt a lil better because I actually lived 45 minutes from the Ville, and I knew a few guys out of that city that Rock knew, so we hit it off well. I didn't have much time to chop it up with Rock that night because I had to get settled in my room before lockdown, which was 9:00 p.m. every night.

That next morning, Rock woke me up around 5:30 a.m. and told me it was time for breakfast. I got up and got myself together, and we struck out when they called chow time for our dorm. Rock began to give me the rundown about this prison. He told me about the race riot that had happened a few months back. He told me that it was about 1,000 Mexicans that rioted against about 200 Blacks, and it was a bloodbath. He told me that's why they were sending a bunch of Blacks out to this prison to balance the numbers out so that it didn't happen that way again. Rock showed me around the yard that morning, and he showed me where to sit in the dining hall. Carolina had one table out of over a hundred, and if it was days that it was packed, like on Thursday, which was chicken day, you had to stand up until one of the Carolina guys got up. You weren't allowed to sit down at any open seat. That could cause a war for the Carolina guys or "car," which is what it's called on the inside.

At Victorville FCI, the cars rolled a little differently than they would run on the East Coast. Out west, we had what they called a south car that consisted of NC, SC, GA, TX, TN, MS, AL, LA, and FL. Every state was responsible for making sure they checked each and every one's paperwork when they got on the yard. Meaning that no one who cooperated with the feds should be walking the yard. As I sat back and watched the structure, I noticed how the staff allowed politics on the yard. What I noticed was that the only race that was divided by states was the Blacks. All the other races were united as a race. The Whites didn't care about what state or city the next White was from; they stuck together as one. Now they did have maybe a divide or two, and that was the White guys who were gang members and those who were not. Other than that, they were one. Same for Mexicans, Cubans, Islanders, and so forth. The Black race was the one so divided. When I noticed the divide, I knew I couldn't be in jail just dealing with my people from Carolina.

I didn't want to be a part of the divide. I had my homeboy, Rock, show me to the Law Library. Foote had already told me to find the inmate lawyer in the Law Library once I got there. He told me I would know who was the best because when you mentioned somebody to help you with law work, they would point you to the best on the yard. Rock introduced me to this old White guy named Tim. Tim told me the first thing I needed to do was get my paperwork. He then told me that if it was clean and I hadn't cooperated with the feds, he would help me with my case. I sent off for my paperwork during my second week on the yard, and it only took about two weeks for me to get it back. By the time I got my paperwork back, I had found out about another inmate that did law work and was a little better than Tim. His name was Naheem from Philly. He was a good Muslim brother with a life sentence. Naheem happened to be in the same dorm that I was in. After getting to know him, I came to find out that Naheem was a heavy guy in the streets of Philly. Even though he was on Muslim time in prison, everyone that came there from Philly had mad love for him. They all looked up to him. After Naheem checked my paperwork to see that I was official, he helped me with my direct appeal. After finding the case law to help with my argument, we put my direct appeal together, and I sent it to the 4th Circuit Court of Appeals. I learned that this appeal process could take anywhere from six months to six years before I would get a decision on my appeal.

While working on my appeal, I can truly say the chains were broken. I had come to the realization that my body was locked up, but the chains were broken from my mind. After digging through case law while working on my appeal, I saw thousands and thousands of cases where the government wronged a defendant. Many were let go from prison, and many were not. The more I read, the more I understood that this was a business and the inmates were just a number. It was a numbers game. While I waited on the decision of my appeal, I never claimed the time the judge had given to me. I wasn't much of a religious type of guy, but while I was waiting in jail to be sentenced, the pastor of my mother's church came to visit me one day out of the blue. I sat down and grabbed the phone on my side of the glass that separated us, and as I did, he picked up his and started to speak. I had probably been to church while he pastored there maybe once, but I had made donations and paid tithes just to keep my mom and aunts happy. As the Rev began to speak to me, I kinda felt awkward because I really didn't believe in religion, so I didn't really understand why he was there. He started to tell me that he knew that I really didn't know him, but he was great friends with my family and the pastor of the church. He went on to say that he had spoken to my mom, and she told him about my situation and how they were recommending 22 years in my case. He then told me that God had spoken to him and told him to deliver this message to me. He told me that God told him to tell me that I wasn't going to do all that time that they were recommending and that even what they ended up giving me, I wasn't going to do all of that time either. That day I prayed with the Rev, and for some reason that day I felt better talking to the Rev than I had talking to my lawyer because when my lawyer was telling me that I wasn't going to get all that time, I wasn't confident in him but for some reason I was with the Rev. It was crazy, but it felt so real. Before leaving, he had told me, no matter what I did, not to claim that time because God had already told him I wouldn't do it all. He also told me that no matter how hard it got for me to not give up on God, He wouldn't give up on me.

So, while serving my time, I never claimed it. If someone asked, I always told them I should be going home soon off my appeal. As I got settled on this prison yard and began to get used to my new life as a prisoner. I began to search for my purpose. I began having talks with God and asking Him to lead me through the tough times that I had in front of me. I became really tight with a few guys while serving time in Victorville FCI II. The first guy that I became close with was a guy by the name of Lil Jeff from Bridgeport, Connecticut. Jeff had been serving time for almost ten years on a twenty-year sentence when I met him. Jeff was well-known around the federal prison system and would introduce me to real stand-up men while doing time with him. It would be

Jeff who helped me through what I called the hardest part of my prison sentence, which was the beginning of it.

The first three years were the hardest part of the prison sentence, but I never let it get the best of me. At one point, I had begun to do a lot of gambling. I was losing around a thousand dollars a week on the poker table. Looking back at it, I realize I was using the card table to cope with my stress. It had become my happy place until one day, I called home to speak with my dad to have him Western Union some money to someone I had lost to on the poker table. This had become a regular thing, but this day, my dad had a conversation with me that would make me start looking at this time a lot differently. This day on the phone, my day told me, "Son, just because you are locked away doesn't mean that your life is over. You are in there spending your money as if you don't have better things to be doing with it." He went on to tell me that I must remember that I still have children out here, and as a man, I must still make sacrifices inside to try and still provide for them. He also went on to remind me that I had properties out here that had to be taken care of, and taxes had to be paid. He told me, "Brandon, don't let the time do you. Continue to fight your case, but most importantly, do all you can to continue to educate yourself so that you are prepared for life after prison." That day, on the phone with my dad, a light bulb went off. I had already begun to read self-help books like *As A Man Thinketh* by James Allen, *Think Like a Champion* by Donald Trump, and *32 Ways to Be a Champion in Business* by Ervin Magic Johnson. Ninety percent of the guys doing time would be reading all the hood novels, and I must admit I tried reading them in the beginning, but it only felt like a waste of time for me. I couldn't get into the hood novels because I had come to the realization that the hood shit was designed to put us in situations like I was currently in. By understanding everything that was going on around me, I was ready to find my purpose because I now knew that sitting on someone's prison yard wasn't it. I had been wrongly over-sentenced, and I realized that success was the only way I could get back at the system that wrongly over-sentenced me and the fake friends who assassinated my character and turned their backs on me after I was sentenced.

Through my observations of other inmates, I noticed that 90% of them were just doing time. Meaning not preparing for their return to the streets. The 90% I'm talking about were the ones that came to prison with nothing and mostly no one. I noticed that most of our loved ones on the outside really didn't understand that the prisons were just one big business and everything cost inside. Anything that was given out for free by the prison was the bare minimum. From the three meals, breakfast, lunch, and dinner, to the hygiene, to the sheets and blankets that were given monthly. So, if you didn't have anyone on the outside who could send you at least $350 a month, then you were almost going to starve. Using the phone cost around $150 a month for 300 minutes. Imagine having kids in different houses and also parents and other close relatives. Three hundred minutes isn't nearly enough to keep family ties strong while away. It even costs inmates to go to see the doctor. Quite naturally, most inmates came straight to prison in search of a good prison job that paid good money so that they could survive. Each job paid differently depending on what department you worked in. The unicor jobs usually paid pretty good. Good enough that most inmates working in unicor made enough money to take care of themselves and send money home to help their families. So instead of having time to really work on themselves and do some soul searching and educating, they are running to the factories on the prison yard every morning from 6:00 a.m. to 3:00 p.m., and if working overtime another shift from 5:00 p.m. to 10:00 p.m. for pennies. Luckily, I was okay with finances. I did hit some hard times over the course of 12 years doing time, but for the most part, I was in a good place financially with the help of my parents, that I didn't have to run and slave for pennies so I could educate myself during my time in prison. The federal prisons offer trade classes where you can get certified in trades like plumbing, electrical, welding, so forth, and so on, but not all federal prisons have trade classes. I have been to a federal prison that didn't have any trade classes that you could get certified in. Most classes were taught by other inmates who had done a trade on the street for a living before their incarceration and were now teaching in prison for an increase in good time. With that being said, the inmates that really wanted to educate themselves while incarcerated had to have a loved one pay for it out of their pocket for them while they were incarcerated, and not many had family that could afford to pay for correspondent college courses for them while they were away. Luckily, I could afford it.

I did take a lot of non-certified computer classes on typing, like Excel and spreadsheets, because I knew that I had to be computer savvy when I returned to society. I followed the news faithfully, and I saw that the world was heading into the information age and technology, and I knew I needed to be prepared. I began by enrolling in college correspondence classes during my first year on the prison yard. I enrolled in business management and remained a student until I was put in for a transfer to another federal prison yard 18 months later.

The prison yard was in West Virginia. It was closer to home than California but still around a 10-hour drive for my family to come to see me. Once on the yard in West Virginia, I realized that the inmates didn't run the prison yard here as they did in California. See, in California, I once had a correctional officer tell me that he respected us inmates because we allowed him to go home every day from work. He told me he would never come to work to make an inmate's life any harder than what they were already going through with this federal system. He respected the inmates, and in return, he got respect back, which was rare because, in just the 18 months that I was there, I saw so many officers get stabbed by inmates. I saw inmates get stabbed and have to get airlifted to ICU, and I had been in a few race riots myself. Now that I was here in West Virginia, I noticed that the respect from the officers was not the same. It was like they came to work just to make inmates' life more stressful than it already was. After getting settled on the prison yard in West Virginia, I enrolled back into college classes. The good thing was that the prison offered free college classes, but there was a waiting list a mile long before you could get into the program, and the list was set up by the earlier release date of the inmate. Since it was the year 2010 and my release date was 2024, I couldn't get into free college courses. Once I figured that out, I decided to take trade classes that I could get certified in. I didn't get into a lot of the things that were going on inside of the prison other than education and becoming one with self and understanding who Brandon was and what was my purpose in life because I knew this wasn't it.

I started all my days off the same. I would get up when they opened the doors at 5:30 a.m. every morning. I would then fix myself a cup of coffee and hit the rec yard on the first move. I would work out from 6:00 a.m. to 8:00 a.m. seven days a week. My homeboys would always ask me why I worked out so much, but what they didn't know is that I had my best talks with God when I was alone on those early mornings in that rec yard. A few of my homeboys would sometimes catch me running the track and talking to myself; well, at least that's what it looked like to them, but what they didn't know was that I was discussing my future daily with God. I had begun to write down a lot of my thoughts and ideas. Through the books I was reading, I learned that your dreams and goals should be written down and filed, so I began doing that. The more I began to take action, the more I realized that the chains were now broken and my future wasn't defined by my present. I may have still been incarcerated physically, but I was now free mentally.

From the beginning of my sentence, I stayed in the Law Library because I knew I had been over-sentenced and had to find the case law to back up my argument. I began to find case law that proved exactly what my argument was. I had been sentenced as a career offender without the proper prior state convictions to lawfully be sentenced as such. The more I began to understand the law, the more I didn't claim the time because I knew I wouldn't stop fighting until I was heard. After maybe six months in West Virginia, I was told by another inmate who came to be like my brother, named Lil Jeff from Connecticut, about a federal prison in Berlin, New Hampshire, that they had just built and was needing inmates from all the other federal prisons to volunteer to come and open the prison up. The thing was that the prison was in the middle of nowhere, and you only got maybe two good months of warm weather. Other than that, it was snow season. So, because of where the prison was, they couldn't get many inmates to volunteer to go. The thing I liked about the new prison was that it was going to have a lot of trade classes that you could get certified in. Mind you, I had only been in West Virginia for six months, so when I went to my case manager to tell him I wanted to volunteer, he quickly told me that I hadn't been on the yard in West Virginia long enough for him to. Typically, before you can ask for a transfer to another jail, you have to be put in for a transfer. He told me that he didn't think his boss would approve the transfer because I was supposed to do at least 18 months on the yard before I could transfer, and even then, I probably wouldn't get a transfer unless my custody level had changed.

However, my case manager still put me in because I told him I wanted those trade classes Berlin would offer. It was almost three months before I was approved and sent off to the prison in Berlin, New Hampshire, but not before having to go through almost two months in transit. The federal system's main transit facility is in Oklahoma City, Oklahoma. It shares the same landing strip as the OKC airport. The federal plane literally pulls right up to the holdover facility, and the 300 inmates are shuffled off the plane right into the facility without our feet ever hitting the ground outside. This was amazing to me, but all I could think of was the money that was being made off of each one of us inmates. To be able to fly 300 inmates around the country in a plane daily let me know that if this was being funded off of taxpayers' dollars, then the government was really mishandling the tax dollars, and I knew that wasn't so.

Here it was: teachers had to take pay cuts because the states couldn't afford to pay them, but here was the federal system paying pilots and marshals great money to fly around the country with inmates. I was extremely baffled by the whole thing. Waiting at this holdover to be transferred to FCI Berlin would be when I would meet a well-known rapper and reality star. It was a crazy encounter, but one I will never forget. I was sitting at the table with a few guys playing spades. I had probably been in the holdover for about two weeks at the time. And every night, there were planes that came in with inmates, and every morning, planes went out with inmates. This particular evening, me and a few guys were sitting playing cards, and around 7:00 p.m. is when the inmates come into the dorms. So, I was sitting there with a few guys who happened to be from New York City. I'm not sure what borough, but I looked up at the guy standing outside of the TV room where other inmates were watching TV. For some reason, I just knew who it was, so I told the guys I was playing cards with who it was. They were like, "Yo, B, you tripping." I'm like, "Yo, I'm willing to bet any of you that's him up there." So, one of the guys from New York hopped up and was like, "I'm going to see what's popping with the homie." Sure enough, it was him when he went up there. See, the situation was crazy with him because they had him in the federal holdover in OKC, where 99% of the inmates were already serving federal prison time and were just here in transit on their way to another prison somewhere in the country and were just waiting to catch a flight with FED Air or were just convicted and on their way to their first prison. The other 1% was designated there to work and help run this big federal airport. Here he was, a known figure in the world here and hadn't even been convicted of a crime yet. The guy couldn't even get on the phone to communicate with his family because he wasn't a convicted federal inmate with a prison number.

In order to use the phones, you had to have a prison number, and he didn't at that point. Just so happened that the young fellow I was playing cards with happened to be from around the same area of NYC. With that being so, my spade partner hit off cool with him and decided to give him a hand with getting in touch with his family. Quite naturally, by his getting tight with him it put me in a position to share the same space with him as well because he started sitting with us for meals and things like that because we had our own little circle that kicked it. During one of our meals or maybe just sitting out in the day room one day, he and I began to have a conversation. For some reason, I think it was just him and

I sitting there that day, but anyway, we started talking about his situation and what he was going through. He started telling me that he hadn't spoken to his family in a few days and couldn't use the phone because he didn't have an inmate number. I told him that the shit was foul how the feds were doing him because he had no business here with us. We were all convicted inmates going to a prison, and he was a man who was being charged with a drug crime and not convicted. The law states innocent until proven guilty, but here, this TV star sat at the table with me, a convicted inmate, and ate the same disgusting meal. Even if he had done what they were charging him with, he still wasn't supposed to be here until after he was convicted. From there, we went to talk about his case a little bit because he had a few questions for me once I had told him that I had been sentenced to almost 16 years for a 69-gram crack cocaine conspiracy. I had told him my issues that I was fighting in court about being over-sentenced. I told him a few things I had learned about federal law since being in the Law Library and fighting my case my whole bid. I ended up breaking down the sentencing scheme the feds had because, at this point on his journey with his case, fam was clueless about this fed shit. For some reason, that day, he got comfortable with me to let me know that he didn't have a clue and was really, for lack of a better word, scared right now. He opened up to me and basically told me that he was guilty and that he just wanted to know how to go about this shit. He told me that the feds had taken like a million or two in jewelry, a drophead phantom, some cash, and a few other things, if I wasn't mistaken. He told me that it was some guys from upstate New York that had set him up and got him caught up in a heroin conspiracy. He kinda told me the details of the situation and asked me if found guilty and what I thought would happen. I broke down the sentencing scheme to him. I explained to him the mandatory minimums and the sentencing enhancements for prior state convictions. By trying to help him figure out what kind of time he would get if convicted, he told me about his past felony conviction. I told him that if he had that violent felony conviction, the federal prosecutor could indict him with an 851 enhancement which would automatically double his mandatory minimum and take the 10-year mandatory sentence he was facing because of the amount of drugs they were alleging in his case to a 20-year mandatory sentence. Then I explained to him how if he had two prior state convictions, he could be considered a career criminal and given a guideline sentence of 262 months to 327 months in federal prison. I was telling him about how they are over-sentencing us at all-time highs. The only way inmates didn't get over-sentenced and light sentences was if they helped the government bring in inmates by being government witnesses to help grow this trillion-dollar slavery empire. I told him not to talk to no one about his case if he planned on fighting because there were a lot of rats walking around in here trying to become government witnesses to go home even after sentencing.

During the few weeks we were together, we spoke about a lot of things, especially the music industry and the reality show. I told him about my entertainment label called 80'Z Baby'Z Ent. I had started before I left and planned on getting back into promoting shows once I won my appeal and came home. Even though I was in prison, I always seized the moment to suck up some game with a man that had really made it out of the hood, a hustler just like myself. We spoke numbers on what he could get his artist to perform at my shows for. Even though I was incarcerated, I was never letting the moment pass me to suck up valuable information and learn something at the same time. He let me in on the business side of the show he was on.

God allowing me to be in the same space with him let me know that what I was going through was just a phase of humbling, growth, and patience for what he had already written for my life. I knew it because, just like when I had met another artist, we instantly became comfortable in each other's presence once we began a conversation, and the same had occurred with he and I. The chains were broken, and mentally, I was now searching for what I knew kept me ahead while I was in the drug game, information. So, after this week or two encounter with him, I knew that I wouldn't go another day in prison without searching for information that could help me to become successful in life when I returned back to society.

CHAPTER

9

DESTINED TO BE GREAT!

After parting with this hip hop star from the holdover terminal, I really knew nothing was stopping me from being a successful entrepreneur and that I was destined to be great. In my mind, after speaking with this reality TV star and building on different subjects such as life and business, nothing he was saying to me was going over my head. We could talk brick talk all the way to corporate talk or stocks and bonds, and I knew what he was saying. I wasn't lost in the conversation or awed because mentally, I was on his level, and I knew that he had one brain, two ears, and one mouth just like me, and if he had accomplished so much legally, I knew I could do the same. Understandably, we knew he had grabbed a bag of money out of the street life, but after talking with this guy, I realized that the brother was intelligent. He wasn't a drug dealer. He was a hustler as I was, so I recognized it. He had done what I was trying to do before I left the streets, managing hip-hop artists and promoting parties.

After leaving OKC, it would be another month in different federal holdover jails in the northern states of the country, like MDC Brooklyn in Brooklyn, NY, and FMC Devens in Massachusetts, before I finally made the bus trip to FCI Berlin in Berlin, New Hampshire along with 29 other inmates. We were the second bus to arrive at this newly built facility that held almost 2,000 inmates. Like every prison in the federal system, when you transfer to another institution, you must go through a week of processing. I happened to end up with a cellmate named Roc, that came on the bus with me. He was from Indianapolis, Indiana, and we became really close. Doing time, it's a must that you have a cellmate that is as low-key and like-minded as you. Having a good celly is key to doing a smooth prison bid. I also had a conversation with an older White guy named Mr. May about politics on the bus ride over to the prison, and I ended up getting a job with him in the education department.

In prison, they make you get a job or go to school. In most cases, 85% of them have to go to school because they don't have a high school diploma or GED; if not, they are required to go to class until they receive it or go home. Most just show up to class with no intention of getting them and never do. In my case, I already had a GED before prison and also a couple of semesters of college. I had vowed never to work in these federal Unicors like a slave. So, if I had to get a job like in this case, because the prison was so new that their trade classes had not started, I went straight to education, where I could spend my day reading and learning. The older White guy, Mr. May, who had come on the bus with me but was in another dorm, happened to get a job in education as well. So, in the beginning, it was just him and I working there. He was the library clerk, and I was the janitor. With him and I working together, we became really close. When I look back on it, it was nothing but God continuing to send his people to educate me while on my journey. I would come to find out by getting close to Mr. May that he was this multi-millionaire lawyer from Dallas, Texas, who had gotten caught up in a 100-million-dollar Ponzi scheme and now was serving three years for it. Mr. May was very educated and taught me a lot about finance, credit, and OPM (other people's money). It would be May that would change the way I looked at finance.

One day, while talking with May, he told me, "Brandon, not being racist, but do you know the difference between us and yall?" Now, he was speaking about rich White people and young, successful Blacks like rappers and ballplayers. I looked at him and told him no. He said, "The difference is that yall go and buy the Ferraris and Bentleys, and we go and lease them in the company name and use it as a write-off for taxes. On top of that, we get the newest model that comes out every few years." Mr. May was onto something here, and he had my attention. He would go on to tell me about the real-estate game and how to start businesses with other people's money, simply by having a business plan and being able to sell an idea to a person who has the money but no idea on how to invest it and make the money work for them. See, while in the drug game on the streets, I always intended to stack enough money to start a business. I never wanted to sell drugs forever. I only wanted to get ahead. Honestly, I wasn't a drug dealer. I was a hustler who happened to get caught up hustling drugs. The problem was that I thought I needed at least half a million to get something going. Silly little me. Mr. May really showed me how to start a business without having not one cent, but only an idea with numbers to back it.

One day, while at work, Mr. May came up to me and asked if I wanted to be the Law Library clerk. I told him that I didn't know about that, but he insisted that I would be good at it because I knew how to work the computers in the Law Library, and I also knew all about case law and filing motions to the courts. He then looked at me and said, "Brandon, you are way more than a janitor." After a few more minutes of thinking, I told him I would do it. He told me to find another inmate to do the janitor job I was doing, and I agreed. Mr. May then asked me to follow him to our boss's office so he could talk to her, and he told me to watch how he did it. I fell in behind May, and we walked right into her office. May took a seat, and I remained standing. He started the conversation with our boss by saying, "Morning, Mrs. Lyons." Mrs. Lyons was a White lady in her fifties. She looked up at him and me, said morning to us, and asked how she could help us. May then looked at Mrs. Lyons and said, "Have you ever heard the saying the billionaire businessmen use when they are embarking on a new business venture? Hire someone smarter than you, get out of their way, and let them build your vision. She replied, and she actually told him that she had heard that before. May replied and told her, "Well, get out of my way and let me build this education department up." He told her he knew she had looked him up and read his file, so she knew he was well-educated and could put all her classes and programs together. Mrs. Lyons looked at him in awe, but I could tell that May had pulled her card because she actually replied and asked where did he plan on starting, and he quickly replied to her and told her that his first course of action was to hire me as a Law Library clerk. Mrs. Lyons quickly asked, "Well, who is going to do the cleaning if he is going to be the law clerk?" May fired back and told her that I had already known somebody who could take my spot and that he and I were going to put a class together to teach new inmates who are coming to prison how to use the computer in the Law Library to research and work on their cases in the appeal courts. She looked at May and me and said that's a great idea. May quickly responded, "Sure it is. I just need for you to get out of my way and let me work," as we exited her office. On the way out, I told May you are the craziest. He said, "No, I'm not. I know exactly what I'm doing.

I would work with May 12 of the 18 months I was at FCI Berlin. May would be the one to tell me about piggybacking off someone's credit while incarcerated so that my credit score would be almost perfect as soon as I walk out of prison. We were talking one day, and I was telling him that I wanted to go home and start a few businesses like a trucking company and nightclub. I wanted to get into real estate, but I didn't know how I was going to get the money to get it going, and I didn't want to go back to the streets. He told me that credit was one way to get started. So he broke down to me how to build my credit from prison. He asked me if I had any family I knew who paid their bills on time and had a decent credit score. I told him my dad did. So, he told me when I went back to my dorm after work to call my dad and ask him to add me to two of his highest credit cards as an authorized user.

At the end of the workday, I quickly went back to the dorm, called my dad, and asked him to add me to his cards. Here it was, just 2011, and I didn't have a release date until 2023, but I'm asking my dad to add me to his cards to build my credit up like I was on my way home then. My dad didn't have many questions, but he told me he would do it. When I got back to work, I made sure to tell May that my dad was going to add me to his cards as an authorized user. When I told him that, he then told me to have a seat beside him and started to teach me how to type out a business plan and explained to me how important knowing how to type up a business plan was if I planned on using OPM to fund any of my businesses. I was all ears because in my mind, coming from the drug game, I looked at OPM as if I was getting kilos of cocaine on consignment from my connect, which in the streets is called fronting, and to get fronted, you needed to know somebody, or you had to have street credit. But in the corporate business world, it was called OPM, and the street cred was a business plan and good credit. Mr. May had really broken down the things I had read in different books like *Rich Dad, Poor Dad*, *Think Like a Champion*, etc. He really made me not just look at finance differently but also at life itself.

The hustling was still in me. It was just something I couldn't control. So, I had to figure out how to transform that energy I had put into selling drugs now into obtaining information so that I could return to society the same energized hustler but not in the same lane. It was now making more sense than ever after having Mr. May come into my life. It takes discipline, humility, and, most importantly, patience to become successful in anything that you do. My goal was to become a student again, but this time, to make sure I learned something every day.

True indeed, I understood business and knew the importance of supply and demand if I didn't understand anything else. Around this time of my prison sentence, I started writing out my short-term and long-term goals for my life. In a lot of the books I had read about successful entrepreneurs, most of them expressed the importance of writing down your goals and plans and also manifesting them into the universe by speaking positivity over your life. I began doing all those things in the second year of my 188-month federal prison sentence. My short-term goal was the first five years of my goals upon my return to society.

At the beginning of my time in jail, I became very cool with this older guy named Pokey from North Carolina, who happened to be fighting his case in the county jail at the same time that I was. We even got sentenced on the same day and even flew together to California to start our Federal prison sentence together at FCI Victorville. Since I had gotten close to Pokey, he always talked about driving 18-wheeler trucks and how he used to be all over the country making money and seeing the world. Pokey started talking to me about the pay and how easy it was to buy you a truck, go into business for yourself, and make a quarter million dollars in a year. He had gotten caught up on his federal case by being at a family member's house when it got raided by the DEA, and he wouldn't cooperate with them, and they tried to make an example out of him for only a half ounce of crack cocaine. Pokey ended up getting twenty years in federal prison after losing in trial. His sentence was overturned on an appeal because he had been over sentenced and ended up only doing five years. However, it would be Pokey that would give me the idea to want to lean toward starting my own trucking company. Before I had been arrested, I had had a friend of mine try to sell me an 18-wheeler, so I knew the price range that I could get one for. So, when I started my five-year goals, I thought to myself, what was a company I could start by using my credit alone the first year of my release? So, trucking is what I had decided on. It wasn't about the money. Trucking was because I knew it was something I wouldn't mind doing myself for a while because I knew that I loved to ride and see different cities because I did it a lot before my arrest.

The next thing on my five-year goals was to get back into promoting parties. I had started 80'Z Baby'Z Ent. Before my arrest, I felt like if I had put all my energy into my parties back then, it would have been a success because of the contacts and friends that I had made in the industry less than a year's time that had started working on my company before my federal indictment. So, party promotion was up next. So, in my five-year goal I was to start a trucking company and promote parties once I got my trucking company up and running. My long-term goals, which were my ten-year goals, were to build onto the trucking company and the entertainment company and to open up a nightclub/event venue so that I would have a place to have my events for my entertainment company. I also wanted to diversify my portfolio with some real estate in my long-term goals and stocks, bonds, and mutual funds with my ten-year goals.

After I finished writing out my short-term and long-term goals, I made copies of them and sent a copy to my father. I kept a copy with me in prison that I read every so often while I was doing my time, but I spoke my goals out into the universe all the time while incarcerated. After about 18 months in FCI Berlin, the opportunity presented itself to me to get a transfer to a federal prison closer to my hometown than I had been in the four years that I had been incarcerated.

Even though I learned to distract myself from the fact that I was doing time by constantly learning and research-ing things for my future, there were still times when I just missed my family, especially my parents, children, nieces, and nephew. My youngest daughter, Jordin, who was one year old, pushed me so much to stay focused while I was incarcerated, and I know she didn't have a clue. My daughter Jordin spent a lot of time with my family, so every time I called home, I spoke to her, and she always would have something new that she would tell me that I owed her when I came home. If it wasn't a trip to Disney World, it was a trip to the beach. She would always tell me I owed her something.

Most importantly, she gave me hope, and even though I was gone away from her, she always reminded me that we had a life to live once this was over. I needed to be prepared for the day I would return because regardless of what, I had one waiting and depending on me to come home and be the

best me I could be. So, after 18 months of taking advantage of all the programs and good men God had sent my way at FCI Berlin, I decided to transfer and get closer to my family to see my children more. The great thing about the 18 months I had spent at FCI Berlin was that I hadn't wasted a day not preparing myself for the streets. I knew that this too shall pass, and after everything was said and done, I was destined to be great.

CHAPTER

10

TIME SERVED

From the time I hit the prison yard in October 2009, I made it my business to feed my mind with positive literature. When I wasn't in the Law Library working on getting out of prison or studying for my college courses, I read books like *As A Man Thinketh* by James Allen and *The Purpose Driven Life* by Rick Warren. Throughout the years, my cellmates would always ask me, "B, why are you reading all those self-help books and shit? I hope they help you when you get out." I would always tell them that I had to try something different than hustling drugs next time around, and I'm just searching for information so I'll be ready when I do get released. In my mind, I could have been going home any day. I had watched thousands of inmates get released from prison over my 12-year span, and I noticed that there was about 85% recidivism. Mostly because they spent all their time in prison still trying to keep up with what was going on in the streets versus keeping up with what was going on with the economy and figuring out a plan to get their life on track so they wouldn't end up back in prison. There were a lot of guys that you could tell were coming back before they had even left because of how they spoke. Seeing that, I chose to extend my vocabulary. Their conversation told you that they still didn't get how this thing called life worked.

It wasn't easy, but there weren't any shortcuts to a good life. The work had to be put in, and I spent my time incarcerated putting the work in so that I was prepared for when my day came to transition back to society. I was always told by the old heads coming up that if you stay ready, you don't have to get ready. The thing about change that I realized was it was necessary to elevate in life. Not being afraid of change and learning to embrace new surroundings and new people were a part of growth. To see a different result in life, I figured out that you had to try different things and separate yourself from those who didn't see life the way you saw it. I had wasted a lot of my time on the streets before, trying to get friends that were around me to see my visions, but the thing about it was that when they didn't see it, I stayed right there with them instead of leaving them there to chase my visions/ dreams. Through my many talks with God over the years of incarceration, I noticed how when you have that relationship with the spirit, it will send folks into your life to help you get past the hurdles that always come when you are en route to the visions He places upon you.

When I got to FCI Edgefield in 2013, I continued to search for information. By being closer to home, I was re- united with some good friends who began to assist me from the free world along the way. One, in particular, helped me write my first business plan by sending me all the information I asked of her to complete my business plan for the lounge/bar I intended on opening within my 10-year goal. Mind you, this was in 2013, and my release date wasn't until 2024. I stayed at Edgefield for almost five years before I was sent to FCI El Reno in Oklahoma on a transfer. FCI El Reno had more trade programs than any prison I had been to in the 11 years I had been in federal prison. I tried my best to get into every program I could get certified in but couldn't get into many because my release date was too far away, and how they picked the classes was by the closest release dates of the inmates that signed up. Luckily, I was able to get into the welding program and complete it. Once I completed the welding program, I was able to slide right into the electrical class because an inmate lost his seat due to discipline.

After doing almost 12 years, the time really began to take a toll on me. I had been fighting my illegal sentence in the Federal Court of Appeals over the past decade, and every motion that I submitted to the court asking for my sentence to be overturned and my case to be looked at for resentencing was denied and shut down. I had submitted one motion that sat on my judge's desk for almost five years. In this motion, I argued that I was wrongly sentenced as a career offender, and I used the case law of United States vs. Simmons, in which his case was identical to mine, and his sentence was overturned. In my case, the United States Attorney for the Middle District of North Carolina agreed with my argument in his rebuttal motion to the courts. In his motion, he agreed that after Simmons' case, I could no longer be sentenced as a career criminal. However, being that I signed a plea agreement, I signed my rights away to argue this over-sentencing issue in my case, and for that reason, I was denied even though if I had been sentenced present day, I could not have received more than five years for the amount of drugs I pled guilty to. I had gotten this news shortly after I got to FCI El Reno, and I never stopped believing that I wouldn't do all this prison time.

Shortly after waiting five years to be denied my appeal, I got some bad news one day on a phone call with my dad. He told me on this phone call that he was diagnosed with prostate cancer. That day on the phone, I felt like I had been hit by a train. At that point, I was just ready to give up on everything I had been working on and preparing for. My parents are my rock, and during this prison bid, I had other friends who were there as well, but nobody like my parents and children. After that phone call, I went back to my cell and asked my cellmate to give me some time alone for a moment. That day, I dropped to my knees, cried my heart out to God, and told him that I couldn't take it in here if my dad were to leave me while I was incarcerated. I had already lost my two nephews, Malik and Derrick, who were like my little brothers. I kept it together for the most part for them, but I couldn't if he had taken my dad too. The old folks always told me that God will not put no more on you than you can bear, and this is my testimony where I can attest to it. Not only did He allow my dad to beat cancer, but He also allowed me to go home with immediate release four years early to live out our last days together on this earth. As I'm writing this, my parents are in their late 70s, still alive and well, and I thank God every day.

President Trump signed into law in 2018 the new retroactive sentencing guidelines for non-violent drug offenders that President Obama signed into law in 2009, meaning it now applied to federal inmates sentenced for drugs before Obama changed the law. I followed the law daily while it was going through the Houses for votes, and once it was ruled in our favor, I instantly filed my motions to the courts. There were a few guys at FCI El Reno I had become real good friends with who had been doing time almost ten years before me and had given up on fighting their sentences. Truth be told, I was on the brink of being the same way, but something wouldn't let me lay down and do all this time that I knew I shouldn't have. So, I took it upon myself to help push them to file their motions because I knew deep in my heart that it was for us this time. My lawyer told me after I was sentenced that I wouldn't do all the time. He told me he had never told a client that, but he told me that he knew there were about to be some changes to the sentencing guidelines for crack cocaine. As all the guys who had been convicted of crack cocaine and I sat back and waited on the federal courts to start releasing us inmates who had been sentenced under these biased and racist sentencing guidelines, I continued to prepare myself for release mentally, physically, and emotionally. I had disciplined myself to get up at 5:00 a.m. every morning to work out and then to class and work. I would then watch TV at the same time every night just to get back up and do it all over again. I set these routines and stuck to them my whole bid because I realized that discipline is the building block of success. I understood that you had to be able to focus mentally and physically and control yourself emotionally to be successful, and all it took was discipline.

A few months after the bill became law, we started to see guys on the prison yard who had non-violent drug charges get immediate release. It seemed like every day for six months straight, someone was going home, but not me. Even the guys I helped get their motions to the court had gone home, and I had yet to hear anything on my case. The United States Attorney, of course, like in all my prior motions I submitted, came back with a rebuttal and a reason why I shouldn't get any relief from my sentence. At one point, after another year of waiting and watching all the other inmates go home who had the same issue as I had, I began to really lose faith, but just before I could, on September 14, 2019, one week before my birthday and one week from the day I was arrested in 2008 I got immediate release. I was taken to a Greyhound bus station in Oklahoma City, Oklahoma, and dropped off at noon with a one-way ticket to North Carolina. I had a lot of people ask me how I felt that day, and I told them all, ready.

Once I made it back to North Carolina, I was instantly visited by people who hadn't thought about me in the last 12 years or at least hadn't let me know they did, and I quickly made it clear I was on something different. That was the discipline I had instilled within me to get me where I was trying to go. The businessman in me did turn a few into pons on the chessboard of my life to get a few steps close to conquering what I had set out to do, but I promise it was only business and nothing personal because I came home with a forgiven heart. I wasn't mad or feeling no way about anything people had said about me or done to me while I was away. My mind was strictly on never allowing myself to be tricked onto the federal slave ship that still exists as a prison and solely on making my and my family's dreams come true. I came home from prison knowing I wanted to go into trucking, so within the first few weeks of being home, I formed my LLC, Integrity Services International, with the help of my best friend. I decided to name my company Integrity because I realized that to prosper, you must have a little integrity in everything you do.

My first job was loading trucks at a warehouse for $10 an hour. It wasn't about the money for me at all. I came home understanding that billion-dollar businesses are built off of OPM (other people's money), and I now knew how to go and get it. I had been building my credit up while incarcerated by piggybacking off my dad's credit, so I came home with a 750 credit score. For the first six months of my release, all I did was work out at 5:00 a.m. every morning, leave the gym and go home and shower, then off to work and be there at 6:30 a.m. every morning 30 minutes early and work all the overtime that they allowed for three months straight.

I always talked with the truck drivers when they came in to get their paperwork for their loads. I would ask questions like where are you taking the load? How much are you making off the load? How are the truck stops? How often do they have problems with their trucks? Etc. My supervisor began to love my work ethic and took a liking to me. I told her my

interest in wanting to drive trucks and that I was looking up schools to go to. She told me she would allow me to have every weekend off even if we had to work if I would take the weekend class and work for her Monday through Friday. That offer worked out great because I needed to keep a job because I planned on using my personal credit to get a personal loan to buy my truck and have the capital to operate my business starting out.

I had figured out that most businesses were built from other people's money (OPM), and I wasn't a stranger to that because, for most of my drug dealing years, I never spent one penny buying drugs. They were all given to me on consignment, and once I sold them, I would pay my suppliers what I owed them, and the rest was mine. In the streets, I had A1 credit because not once did I fail to pay back what I owed, and for that reason, I was never without product. I learned early that being a stand-up man took you a long way. After years of sitting in prison, studying business, and taking college courses in marketing, I realized that the business world was run off the same model. It wasn't about having a bunch of money; it was about having the right ideas and the right business plans because there's always someone who is looking to invest.

A few weeks after my release, I started working, and I worked every day. I started truck driving school three months after my release from prison, in which I used the credit card I had obtained to foot the bill. Preparing my credit before my release had already paid off. It took me three months to finish trucking school because I only went on the weekends. Once I finished, I immediately took a trucking position driving for a company based in Charlotte, NC. Shortly after, I used my credit to take out a personal line of credit to purchase my first truck while continuing to drive for different trucking companies to gain the experience I needed to feel comfortable enough to get into my own truck. While working for these other companies, it wasn't just about the driving experience; I was paying attention to the inner workings of the companies. From the shipping managers to the dispatchers, I asked questions to understand their positions and their value to the company. So, while I was driving and getting experience on the driving side, I was studying the dispatching and brokering side of the business as well.

While all of this was going on, I had become a student under an old friend of mine who had his own trucking company. He was very well-versed when it came to the maintenance side of the trucking business. In trucking, one of your biggest expenses is maintenance, so to survive the first two years, you must be able to handle the maintenance. By having a friend in the business, I was able not only to learn how to work on my own truck enough to save my company some money but also I was able to meet different mechanics. He introduced me to some good ones who were reasonably priced. Understanding how important maintenance was, I locked in with a good mechanic who, to this day, does weekly routine checks on my trucks and is also on call when there is an emergency that needs to happen. To be successful in trucking, it's a must that you have a great mechanic putting his hands on your truck weekly, even if it's just making sure all tire pressures are right. I became focused on being the best at this trucking business, and I searched for all the information necessary to be just that: the best.

In October 2020, one year after my release from prison, I became the owner and operator of my own trucking company, Integrity Services International, LLC dba Integrity Trucking. For the next few years, I would live in my truck, learning everything there is to know about the trucking world. By the end of 2021, not only had I added another unit to my trucking company, but I also started my second company, Royalty Logistics International, LLC dba Royalty Logistics Group, which is my freight management company. Coming from the streets, I always had a team with me because I realized early on that you can't do anything alone. I had run into a lot of guys who embarked on the journey of trucking and were doing it alone. Ninety-seven percent of them were having it hard and barely making it. Seeing that gave me more ideas, being that I had a team with me that I had trained very well, and we had the capability to help other trucking companies that were just starting out by offering them dispatch services. After that, we began to offer fleet management services to other companies. Within this one field, I figured out a way to generate five different streams of income in different parts of the logistics world. Within my first year of business, I grossed 350K, and within my second year of business, we were able to gross almost one million dollars in the logistics world from the comforts of my home office. Within two years, I had diversified my business portfolio into several streams of income, including commercial property, money market accounts, and cryptocurrency.

In 2010, I was in federal prison for two years. However, I had already written out my five-year short-term goals but also my long-term goals as well. Nevertheless, there is so much more on the horizon for Integrity Services International, LLC and Royalty Logistics International, LLC. It was a long journey for me, so I decided to write this book to shed light on the ten percent of people who may start life off wrong but get it right before it's too late and finish strong. I also wanted to give other inmates that I left behind a blueprint on how to do the time and not let the time make them give up on their dreams. Too many people get it wrong and are convinced by foolish people around them that just because they have felonies on their record, they are limited to doing things, which in turn keeps them from progressing in life to their fullest potential. But I am a living witness that you can do anything that you put your mind to. I am not where I want to be, but I'm a lot further from where the odds predicted I would be.

Despite the enormous light shed on recidivism rates of inmates returning to prison, Integrity Services International LLC has expanded its vision to change the narrative in the urban communities. We are continuously working hard to establish entities and resources to help others transition into entrepreneurship and successful careers. The following resources are only the beginning of what is yet to come. Stay tuned!

Chosen One Inc. is a non-profit organization I established to help vulnerable populations such as children, older adults, and those transitioning home from prison. Through our non-profit, we help with various needs depending on the funding. Chosen One Inc. representatives can be contacted at IntegrityServicesInt@gmail.com.

Through the experience and knowledge gained from running a successful trucking company and freight brokering company, I began helping others embark into the logistics industry. To learn more about the services we offer, visit http://integrityservicesinternational.com.

www.ingramcontent.com/pod-product-compliance
Lightning Source LLC
Chambersburg PA
CBHW030312130626
46549CB00002B/826